Food Processor Cookbook

By The Editors of Consumer Guide®

A Fireside Book Published by Simon and Schuster

Table of Contents

A Fireside Book
Published by Simon and Schuster
A Gulf+Western Company
Rockefeller Center, 630 Fifth Avenue
New York, New York 10020

Manufactured in the United States of America
7   8   9   10

Library of Congress Cataloging in Publication Data
Main entry under title:

Food processor cookbook.
   (A Fireside book)
   Includes index.
   1. Cookery.   2. Kitchen utensils.   I. Consumer guide.

TX652.F6   641.5'89   76-46993
ISBN 0-671-22675-4
ISBN 0-671-22676-2 pbk.

Table of Contents

Photo Credits: Bill Miller; American Dairy Association; American Mushroom Institute; California Apricot Advisory Board; California Fresh Peach Advisory Board; California Raisin Advisory Board; Florida Celery Commission; and Wheat Flour Institute.

Cover Photo: Bill Miller
Cover Design: Frank E. Peiler

Introduction

THE KITCHEN renaissance continues to flourish. Experienced cooks and novices are attempting epicurean feasts, sampling ethnic specialties from around the world, and perfecting treasured family recipes. Exotic spices and unusual fruits and vegetables appear on more and more tables as the spirit of culinary adventure inspires the family "chef" to new discoveries.

Naturally, the adventuresome cook is also looking for shorter, more efficient ways to make her or his culinary discoveries. In the search for time-saving kitchen techniques, the multipurpose food processor opens a veritable new world of cooking possibilities.

Multipurpose food processors come in two basic types. There is the free-standing, multipurpose machine that has a power base and various attachments—a blender, a grinder, a shredder/slicer, a dough hook and so forth. There is also the Cuisinart-type of food processor that can handle blending, shredding, slicing and other tasks with only the change of a blade.

The differences between Cuisinart-type food processors and multipurpose machines lie in the space each occupies, the cost and the job each can perform. Multipurpose machines have attachments which can add over $500 to the total cost of the unit; but a completely equipped heavy-duty mixer can do almost any food preparation task.

If you do not already own one of these two types of kitchen machines, turn to the last chapter for test reports. Nearly every manufacturer of small kitchen appliances now has a version of the Cuisinart food processor. Performance of the Cuisinart imitators ranges from elegantly efficient to barely acceptable.

Both types of kitchen machines can do the work of a skilled pair of hands wielding a finely honed chef's knife, whisk or cleaver. They liberate the gourmet and the everyday cook from all kinds of tedious cooking tasks. The FOOD PROCESSOR COOKBOOK is designed to introduce you to all the revolutionary cooking techniques made possible with a multipurpose machine.

The kitchen-tested recipes in this book include gourmet specialties, everyday favorites and recipes for entertaining. A Pâté de Foie à la Crème looks gorgeous and complicated to make—but it is not. All you have to do is follow the pictures in the chapter on Appetizers and you will have it made before you can worry about it. To round out your soup repertoire, turn to the Soup chapter for a spicy Gazpacho, an elegant Chilled Mushroom Bisque, or an Oeufs Poché Potage (Poached Egg Soup). You will be inspired with the Salad chapter, too. Vegetables can be evenly sliced, chopped or shredded in an instant for the incomparable Marinated Fresh Vegetables, the Hot Seafood Salad and the Moroccan Salad. Of course, your exquisite salad creations deserve exquisite dressings. Mayonnaise, Thousand Island and Green Goddess Dressings are foolproof when you follow the photographs in the Dressings chapter.

In the Main Dish chapter, you will find recipes suitable for a formal dinner, as well as recipes perfect for casual occasions. You will want to try the Beef and Mushroom Ratatouille for a Mediterranean specialty; and perhaps serve the Orange Raisin Stuffed Lamb Roll for an impressive Sunday dinner.

Alongside the main dishes, you will find a supporting cast of delightful vegetable dishes, breads, sauces, relishes and beverages. Who could resist plucking out a Brioche's topknot, dabbing it with butter and eating it without further ceremony?

And for dessert? Even working people will have time to make their favorite brownies, cakes or pies. If Cream Puffs filled with Almond Cream are not rich enough for you, try the Chocolate Mousse with Chocolate Sauce. Recipes as luscious and rich as these should not be so simple to make!

Working with a Multipurpose Food Processor

Adding a Cuisinart-type food processor or other multipurpose machine to your life is just like adding another person—you will be happiest if you begin with respect and more than a passing acquaintance, followed by a period of adaptation. Thoroughly study the instructions that come with the machine and keep the general instructions in mind when working with the recipes in this book. Certain machines have some restrictions on what they can and cannot do, and it is important to know these limitations before you start.

Most of the Cuisinart-type machines have slicing, shredding and cutting blades, with the cutting blade used for mixing, kneading, grating, chopping and puréeing. Some have more abilities than these, some less. The Cuisinart, for example, has a French fry cutter, a fine shredding blade, a fine slicing blade and an optional juice extractor attachment. La Machine can chop, slice, shred, etc., but cannot mix. GE's processor cannot handle yeast doughs.

When you first acquire a food processor, keep the machine out on the counter, if possible, and make a special effort to use it. Doing all kitchen tasks laboriously by hand is a habit that is hard to break; but, once you have made the adjustment, you will find it hard to return to chopping, slicing, mixing or grinding by hand.

Safety

The most dangerous parts of Cuisinart-type food processors are the razor sharp blades. Handle them with care when you unpack them, use them and clean them. You can give yourself a nasty cut groping in soapy water for a blade. A blade rack to store the blades neatly and safely is a wise purchase.

Always wait until the blade has stopped moving before taking off the cover. Always use the pusher to insert food down the feed chute. Some Cuisinart-type processors have braking action to stop the blades more quickly. Braking action is a recommended safety feature.

The cover lock mechanism is another safety feature. All the Cuisinart-type processors must have the cover tightly in position before they can be used. Still, there is nothing (except good sense) to prevent you from sticking fingers down the feed chute while the motor is running. These appliances should be strictly off-limits to children. Pulse switches are featured on many of the newer Cuisinart-type machines. On some models you just turn the machine's top in short bursts. We think the top-operated mechanism is just as easy, if not easier, than an additional switch on the base. In our tests we found that it was so easy to move the switch from "pulse" to "on" that we had some processors going when we wanted them off.

Most Cuisinart-type food processors have an automatic temperature control that cuts out the motor when it gets too hot. It is important to turn the operating switch off when the motor cuts out. Otherwise you might walk away, planning to come back soon, only to find the motor has come back on when it cooled down.

Working with the Recipes

Throughout the recipes in this book you will find references to both types of multipurpose food processors. Each chapter has one or two recipes with photographed directions that illustrate the basic food processor techniques. Each of the recipes that follows has an introduction that tells which blade of a Cuisinart-type food processor or which attachment of a multipurpose machine is used in the recipe. For example, when the recipe's directions call for chopping, the recipe's introduction will say something like, "the chopping can be done with a food processor's steel blade or with a multipurpose machine's blender." If more than one blade or attachment is required, that is also mentioned in the recipe's introduction. The term "food processor" refers to a Cuisinart-type machine; and "multipurpose machine" refers to an appliance like the Bosch, Braun, KitchenAid, and so forth. Sometimes there are steps that should not be done with a Cuisinart-type machine. In some recipes, whipping cream or egg whites should be done with a mixer. (You could use an electric mixer, a rotary beater or a wire whisk.) Some machines slice soft foods, like tomatoes, better than other machines. You have to know what your food processor can and cannot do—in some recipes it does not matter if the tomatoes are slightly squashed; in other recipes, you may want to cut the tomatoes by hand.

Food prepared with love and creativity is enjoyed the most. The FOOD PROCESSOR COOKBOOK has been written to help women and men, young and old, enjoy a new world of culinary pleasure. Happy cooking!

Appetizers

As preludes to formal dinners or star attractions at cocktail parties, appetizers are irresistible tasty morsels. They pique the appetite, signaling the beginning of a pleasurable time with good friends and good food.

Pâté de Foie à la Crème

Pâté de Foie à la Crème

A twin treat, this handsome appetizer displays a layer of savory chicken liver pâté on the bottom and a layer of Madeira-flavored cream cheese on the top. You can make the garnish as elaborate or as simple as you wish, using cut pimiento for flowers and thin slices of green pepper for stems.

Chilled Crème
- 1 teaspoon unflavored gelatin
- 3 tablespoons water
- 2 packages (3 ounces each) cream cheese, cut in chunks
- 1 can (13 ounces) consommé, chilled
- 1 tablespoon Madeira

Pâté
- 1 cup butter, divided
- 1 onion, peeled and quartered
- 1 teaspoon dry mustard
- ½ teaspoon salt
- ¼ teaspoon curry powder
- ¼ teaspoon ground cloves
- ⅛ teaspoon ground pepper
  Dash cayenne pepper
- 1 pound chicken livers
- 1 teaspoon unflavored gelatin
- 3 tablespoons water
- ½ cup whipping cream
- 2 tablespoons Cognac or Madeira

Chilled Crème
1. Sprinkle the gelatin over the water in a small saucepan.
2. Heat the gelatin over low heat until it dissolves. Cool.
3. Add the gelatin, cream cheese, consommé and Madeira to a processor or blender container and blend until smooth.
4. Butter an 8-inch, round cake pan. Line it with waxed paper and butter the paper.
5. Pour in the cheese-consommé mixture. Cover it with plastic wrap and chill until firm.

Pâté
6. Meanwhile, prepare the pâté by melting ½ cup of the butter in a skillet or saucepan.
7. Add the onion, dry mustard, salt, curry, cloves, pepper and cayenne. Cook and stir over medium heat until the onion is tender.
8. Add the chicken livers and cook and stir until they are no longer pink.
9. Turn the chicken liver mixture into a processor or blender container and blend until smooth.
10. Sprinkle the gelatin over the water in a small saucepan.
11. Heat the gelatin over low heat until it dissolves. Cool.
12. Add the cream, Cognac, and the remaining ½ cup butter, cut in chunks, to the liver in the processor.
13. Add the cooled gelatin to the liver mixture in the processor and blend until smooth.
14. Remove the plastic wrap from the chilled crème in the pan and pour the chicken liver mixture over it. Cover the pâté with plastic wrap and chill for several hours.
15. To serve, uncover the pâté and invert it onto a serving platter. Garnish it with green pepper and pimiento, if desired.

Makes 25 to 30 appetizer servings

First, prepare the layer of chilled crème. With the plastic blade in place, put the dissolved cooled gelatin, consommé and Madeira in the processor container. Add the chunks of cream cheese.

Blend the crème ingredients until smooth. Have ready a buttered and paper-lined round pan. Pour the crème into the pan and cover it with plastic wrap. Chill until firm.

While the crème chills, begin preparing the pâté layer by melting the first ½ cup butter in a skillet or saucepan and adding the quartered onion and all the seasonings. Cook and stir over medium heat until the onion is tender.

Add the chicken livers to the seasoned onion mixture. Cook and stir until the livers are no longer pink.

Turn the chicken liver and onion mixture into the processor container and blend until smooth, using the steel blade,

Prepare the gelatin. While it cools, add the cream, Cognac, and last ½ cup butter, cut into chunks, to the liver in the processor. Add the ingredients through the feed tube while the processor is running. Add the cooled gelatin to the pâté mixture and blend until smooth.

Remove the plastic wrap from the chilled layer of crème and pour the pâté over the creme. Cover it with plastic wrap and chill thoroughly before inverting on a serving platter. Garnish with green pepper and pimiento, if you wish.

Quiche au Roquefort

Since appetizers have to compete with cocktails, assertive flavors often are the biggest hits. Quiche au Roquefort fits the bill: it can be tasted over a martini and is irresistible. This quiche combines a nippy cheese flavor with velvet-smooth texture; it can be served hot or cold. The filling may be prepared in a food processor or the blender container of other machines.

9 inch pastry shell (see Rich Processor Pastry)
1 cup light cream or half-and-half
4 ounces cream cheese
4 ounces Roquefort cheese
3 eggs
4 green onions, cut in short lengths
¼ teaspoon salt
¼ teaspoon white pepper

1. Using a pie pan or flan dish, bake the pastry shell in a 375°F oven for 5 minutes.
2. Meanwhile, blend the cream, cream cheese, Roquefort and eggs until smooth. Add the onions and seasonings and blend until the onions are chopped.
3. Pour the filling into the partially-baked pie shell and return it to the oven for 30 to 35 minutes or until a knife inserted near the center comes out clean.
4. Cool the quiche 5 to 10 minutes before cutting it into thin wedges. Serve warm or chilled.

Makes 18 appetizer servings

For a 9½-inch flan dish, use the following amounts: 1¾ cup light cream or half and half, 8 ounces cream cheese, 6 ounces Roquefort, and 5 eggs.

Rich Processor Pastry (Pâté Brisée)

With a food processor to handle the tricky mixing, anyone can turn out a feather-light, rich pastry shell for a favorite quiche, a special pie or tarts. The only thing the processor cannot do is roll out the dough. For Quiche au Roquefort you will need only half of this recipe; refrigerate the rest to use for other dishes. (This recipe also may be made in the blender container of a multipurpose machine: combine the flour and butter in the blender container; mix the water in by hand.)

2 cups all-purpose flour
½ teaspoon salt
⅔ cup very cold or frozen butter, cut in chunks
¼ cup ice water

1. Measure the flour and salt into the processor.
2. Add the butter chunks and mix by turning the motor on and off in short bursts, until the mixture is the consistency of coarse meal.
3. With the motor running, pour the ice water in through the feed tube and mix until the dough forms a ball. If the dough seems too soft, add a tablespoon or so more of the flour and mix until incorporated.
4. Roll out the dough to the desired size and thickness on a lightly floured surface. Refrigerate any leftover dough to use for tarts and other pastries.

Makes enough pastry for a double crust, 9-inch pie

Measure all ingredients for the pastry crust and set them out together next to the processor. Mixing will take only seconds. Use the steel blade in the processor throughout this recipe.

Put the measured flour and salt into the processor. Cut frozen or very cold butter into chunks. Add the chunks and mix by turning the motor on and off in short bursts. The mixture is done when it is the consistency of meal.

With the motor running, pour the ice water through the feed tube and mix until the dough forms a ball. If the dough seems too soft, add another tablespoon of flour and mix until the flour is incorporated.

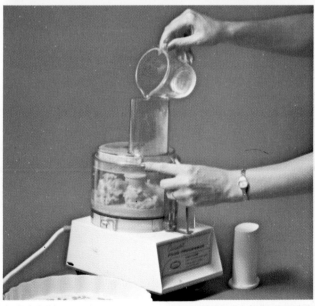

Remove the dough from the processor container. The dough will be cold and ready to roll out without further chilling.

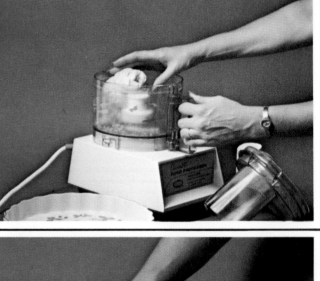

On a lightly floured surface, roll out the dough to a circle about 2 inches larger in diameter than the pie plate or flan dish to be used.

Bake the pastry shell in a preheated 375°F oven for 5 minutes. To prevent the pastry from puffing, line the raw shell with waxed paper and top the paper with dried beans, peas or rice. While the shell bakes, assemble all the ingredients for the quiche filling.

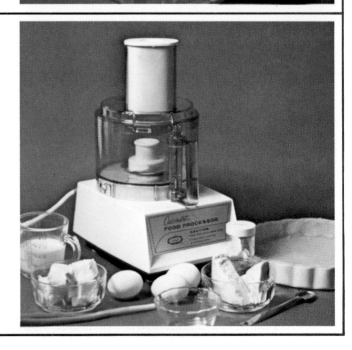

Put the cream, cream cheese, Roquefort and eggs in the processor and blend until smooth, using the steel blade.

While the machine is running, add the cut-up onions, salt and pepper through the feed tube. Blend until they are chopped.

Pour the cheese mixture into the partially-baked pie shell. Bake for 30 to 35 minutes or until a knife inserted near the center comes out clean.

Quiche au Roquefort

Steak Tartare

Steak Tartare

A sophisticated appetizer for sophisticated tastes, Steak Tartare is best and safest when you grind the steak at home, immediately before serving. The steel blade of a processor or grinding attachment of a multipurpose machine makes grinding the steak easy.

1 small onion, peeled and
    quartered
1 pound lean, tender beef
    (tenderloin or sirloin)
1 egg
4 anchovies (optional)
2 sprigs parsley
4 teaspoons capers, drained
    Dash hot pepper sauce
½ teaspoon Worcestershire sauce
½ teaspoon salt
    Generous dash freshly ground
      black pepper

Garnish
4 egg yolks
2 tablespoons capers
1 medium onion, chopped

1. Chop the onion in the food processor or in a blender container.
2. Trim the beef of all fat and sinew. Cut it into chunks. Add ½ of the meat to the processor or grinder. Add ½ of the remaining ingredients and chop by turning the motor on and off in short bursts until the meat is coarsely ground. Do not overprocess. Turn the meat into a medium-sized bowl.
3. Repeat the chopping or grinding with the remaining meat and remaining ingredients. Combine the mixtures in the bowl, mixing gently.
4. Form the beef into 4 patties and make a small depression in the center of each to hold the egg yolk.
5. Serve with an egg yolk in the center of each patty and sprinkle the patties with the 2 tablespoons of capers and chopped onion. Serve the steak with crackers, thin bread or toast.

Makes 4 patties

Sunshine Fruit Tray

Think of this fruit and cheese dip when you want an exotic, spicy appetizer, a snack or even a dessert. The processor's steel blade or a blender makes mixing the dip effortless.

2 cups cottage cheese
¼ cup golden raisins
¼ cup chutney
2 teaspoons lemon juice
1 teaspoon curry powder
    Fresh fruit slices
    Lemon juice

1. Combine all the ingredients in the food processor or blender container and blend until the cottage cheese is smooth and the raisins and chutney are finely chopped.
2. Serve the dip with sliced fresh fruit. Brush or sprinkle the fruit slices with lemon juice to prevent darkening.

Makes about 2¼ cups dip

Sunshine Fruit Tray, Snack Pasties and Lazy Day Tacos

Snack Pasties

A portable nibble for patio parties or snacking, these pasties are scrumptious miniature turnovers. Use the shredding blade of any machine to take care of shredding the cheese.

4 ounces Cheddar cheese, chilled
1 can (15½ ounces) corned beef hash
1 can (8½ ounces) crushed pineapple, drained
1 tablespoon prepared horseradish
1 package (9.5 ounces) refrigerated buttermilk flaky biscuits

1. Shred the cheese.
2. Combine the cheese with the hash, pineapple and horseradish.
3. On a lightly floured surface, roll each biscuit into a 5-inch circle. Place about ¼ cup corned beef mixture on half of biscuit, leaving an edge of pastry for sealing. Fold the pastry in half.
4. Seal the edges with the tines of a fork. Prick the tops with a fork.
5. Arrange them on baking sheets and let them stand 15 minutes.
6. Bake in a preheated 400°F oven 10 to 15 minutes or until golden brown.

Makes 10 pasties

Lazy Day Tacos

Tacos with a difference! These appetizers are filled with a savory tuna salad — delicious for snacks on the patio. Your multipurpose machine's or food processor's shredding and slicing blades will justify this recipe's name.

6 ounces Cheddar cheese, chilled
3 stalks celery
½ cup pitted black olives
⅓ medium head lettuce
1 can (9½ ounces) tuna, drained and flaked
¾ cup dairy sour cream
1 tablespoon instant minced onion
1 teaspoon chili powder
½ teaspoon salt
10 taco shells prepared according to package directions

1. Shred the cheese using the shredding blade of the food processor or multipurpose machine. Set the cheese aside.
2. Switch to the slicing blade and slice the celery and olives. Set them aside.
3. Slice the lettuce and set it aside.
4. In a medium-sized bowl, combine the celery and olives with the tuna, sour cream, onion, chili powder and salt.
5. Spoon a layer of lettuce into the taco shells, then fill each with about ¼ cup of the tuna mixture.
6. Sprinkle about 2 tablespoons of the shredded Cheddar cheese in each taco.

Makes 10 tacos

Swiss Cheese Fondue

Swiss Cheese Fondue

Almost nothing helps guests get better acquainted than dipping into a pot of rich fondue. Shredding the cheeses is effortless when you use the shredding blade of the food processor or multipurpose machine.

8 ounces Emmentaler (Swiss) cheese, chilled
8 ounces Gruyére cheese, chilled
1½ cups Moselle wine or vermouth
½ clove garlic
2 tablespoons butter
¼ teaspoon nutmeg
1 tablespoon cornstarch
2 tablespoons Cointreau or Kirsch
½ teaspoon salt
Dash pepper
1 loaf French bread, cubed

1. Shred the chilled cheeses using the shredding blade of the food processor or multipurpose machine.
2. Simmer the wine, garlic, butter and nutmeg in a saucepan until the wine is reduced slightly.
3. Add the cheeses ⅓ at a time; stir constantly with a wooden spoon until the cheeses are melted and blended.
4. Mix the cornstarch, Cointreau, salt and pepper. Bring the fondue to a boil and add the Cointreau mixture. Mix well.
5. Pour the fondue into a chafing dish or fondue pot and heat until bubbly.
6. Reduce the heat and let each guest dip bread cubes into the fondue with long-handled forks.

Makes about 3 ⅔ cups

Wisconsin Cheese Crock

Find several small crocks or bowls, then make a double or triple batch of this nippy cheese and fill the little crocks or bowls to keep on hand in the refrigerator for parties or special gifts. Do all the mixing in the food processor with the steel blade or in the blender container of a multipurpose machine.

1 package (8 ounces) cream cheese
4 ounces blue cheese
¼ cup mayonnaise
2 or 3 sprigs parsley
1 teaspoon Worcestershire sauce
2 ounces walnuts, toasted

1. Combine the cheeses, mayonnaise, parsley and Worcestershire and blend until smooth.
2. Add the walnuts and mix just until coarsely chopped.
3. Pack the cheese into a crock or small bowl, cover tightly and chill several hours to blend the flavors.

Makes about 2 cups

Appetizers

Shrimp Balls in Sweet-Sour Tomato Sauce

If your cocktail party needs a friendly focal center, set out a chafing dish of these sweet-sour shrimp morsels and watch your guests enjoy sampling them. The secret crunch inside each ball is half a water chestnut. Making bread crumbs and chopping and blending ingredients is done in a flash with the food processor's steel blade or in the blender container of a multipurpose machine.

Shrimp Balls
- 3 or 4 slices day-old bread (to make 1 cup crumbs)
- 1 pound cooked shrimp
- 1 onion, peeled and quartered
- 2 cloves garlic
- 2 eggs
- 1 tablespoon Worcestershire sauce
- 2 sprigs parsley
- 2 green onions, cut in short lengths
- ½ teaspoon salt
  Dash pepper
- 12 water chestnuts, drained and halved
  Batter
  Fat or oil for deep frying
  Sweet-Sour Tomato Sauce

Batter
- ½ cup all-purpose flour
- ½ cup milk
- 1 slice (1 inch thick) onion
- ½ teaspoon baking powder
- ½ teaspoon sugar
- ½ teaspoon salt

Sweet-Sour Tomato Sauce
- 1 small onion, peeled
- 3 tablespoons butter
- ¼ cup all-purpose flour
- 2 cups chicken broth
- ⅓ cup packed brown sugar
- ⅓ cup vinegar
- ¼ cup catsup
- 1 tablespoon soy sauce

Shrimp Balls
1. Tear the bread into pieces. Make crumbs in the food processor or blender container. You will need 1 cup of fine crumbs. Remove the crumbs and set them aside.
2. Coarsely chop the shrimp, onion and garlic using the food processor or blender. Turn the chopped mixture into a medium-sized bowl.
3. Put the eggs, Worcestershire sauce, parsley, green onions, salt and pepper in the processor or blender container. Blend until almost smooth.
4. Lightly mix together the bread crumbs, shrimp and egg mixtures.
5. Form the mixture into small balls, the size of walnuts. Make an indentation and push ½ a water chestnut into each ball.
6. Dip the balls into the batter.
7. Fry until lightly browned in deep fat that has been preheated to 350°F-375°F.
8. Place the balls in a chafing dish and spoon the Sweet-Sour Tomato Sauce over the top. Serve with appetizer picks.

Makes 2 dozen

Batter
1. Place all the ingredients in the food processor or blender container.
2. Blend until the onion is finely chopped.
3. Pour the batter into a small bowl.

Sweet-Sour Tomato Sauce
1. Slice the onion with the slicing blade of the food processor or multipurpose machine.
2. Sauté the onion in the butter in a medium-sized skillet until tender. Add the flour; cook and stir over medium heat about 2 minutes.
3. Add the chicken broth; cook and stir until the mixture comes to a boil and is smooth and thickened.
4. Add the remaining ingredients; cook and stir until smooth and thickened.

Makes about 2 cups

Cheddar Shrimp Triangles

You can prepare these zesty, bite-sized appetizers ahead of time. They are also good along with a luncheon soup or as a snack. Use the shredding blade of the food processor or multipurpose machine for the cheese; use the processor's steel blade or a blender for the chopping.

- 4 ounces Cheddar cheese, chilled
- 1 can (4½ ounces) medium shrimp, drained and rinsed
- ¼ medium green pepper, seeded
- ¼ small onion, peeled
- ⅛ teaspoon basil
- 8 slices sandwich bread, toasted
  Softened butter
  Pimiento-stuffed olives, sliced

1. Shred the cheese and set it aside.
2. Coarsely chop the shrimp, green pepper and onion.
3. Add the shrimp and vegetables to the cheese along with the basil and mix.
4. Trim the crusts from the toast. Spread the toast with butter.
5. Spread the cheese-shrimp mixture on the toast. Cut each slice crosswise to form 4 triangles.
6. Garnish with the olive slices.

Makes 32 triangles

Hot Mexican Bean Dip

Use your own leftover refried beans or buy canned "refritos" for this simple but spunky dip. Vegetable chunks or tortilla chips are the obvious dunkers.

2 cups refried beans or 1 can (16 ounces)
4 ounces Cheddar, Longhorn or Monterey Jack cheese
1 can (4 ounces) mild green chilies, drained
1 medium onion, peeled and quartered

1. Combine all the ingredients in the food processor or blender container of a multipurpose machine and blend until the cheese is coarsely shredded.
2. Pour the dip into a saucepan or chafing dish and heat until the cheese melts. Serve hot.

Makes about 2½ cups dip

Tangy Vegetable Dip

Set out a bowl of this dip with fresh vegetable pieces *(crudites),* assorted crackers or wafers, or sliced, fresh apples or pears. Tangy Vegetable Dip can double as a sauce; heat and spoon it over fresh, steamed vegetables. Use the steel blade of the food processor or prepare the vegetables in the blender container of a multipurpose machine.

2 medium carrots, peeled and cut in short lengths
½ medium green pepper, seeded
½ small onion, peeled
1 cup cottage cheese
⅓ cup barbecue sauce
1 teaspoon lemon juice
½ teaspoon salt
½ teaspoon sugar
½ teaspoon pepper

1. Shred or coarsely chop the carrots, green pepper and onion.
2. Add remaining ingredients and mix just until smooth.
3. Cover and chill until ready to serve.

Makes about 1½ cups dip

Hot Mexican Bean Dip   **Tangy Vegetable Dip**

Appetizers

Mr. McGregor's Garden Dip

This dip has a delightful tangy flavor that creates a perfect appetizer when served with crisp, garden vegetable dippers. The whole recipe is mixed in a few seconds using the food processor's steel blade or the blender container of a multipurpose machine.

1 small onion, peeled and quartered
1 cup cottage cheese
1 package (3 ounces) cream cheese, chunked
1 tablespoon lemon juice
1 teaspoon prepared horseradish
1 teaspoon celery salt
¼ teaspoon dry mustard
1 vegetable bouillon cube, crushed, or 1 packet vegetable broth base

1. Chop the onion finely in the food processor or blender.
2. Add the remaining ingredients. Blend until smooth.

Makes about 1⅓ cups

Mid-East Eggplant Appetizer

Looking for an unusual opener? Eggplant with vegetables makes a unique, exotic spread. Serve the dip with sesame seed wafers to complete the Middle Eastern flavor. The food processor's steel blade or the slicing blade of a multipurpose machine will have the vegetables chopped in an instant.

2 small or 1 large eggplant
2 tomatoes
1 large onion, peeled and quartered
1 green pepper, seeded
½ pound mushrooms
2 cloves garlic
½ cup olive oil
2 cups tomato sauce
1 tablespoon vinegar
1 teaspoon sugar
1 teaspoon basil
½ teaspoon salt

1. Cut a thin slice lengthwise off one side of each eggplant to form an eggplant "boat."
2. Scoop out the meat, leaving a ¼-inch thick shell. Cover the shells and chill them.
3. Chop or slice the eggplant, tomatoes, onion, green pepper, mushrooms and garlic.
4. Heat the olive oil in a large skillet or saucepan. Add the vegetables and cook and stir over medium-high heat for 3 to 4 minutes.
5. Stir in the tomato sauce, vinegar, sugar, basil and salt. Simmer uncovered about 30 minutes or until thick.
6. Chill the vegetables. To serve, spoon the mixture into the eggplant shells.

Makes about 3½ cups

Mid-East Eggplant Appetizer

Ham and Cheese Snacks

Surprise guests? You can serve this hearty appetizer in no time. Let the food processor's steel blade or a blender do the work.

1 can (4½ ounces) deviled ham
¼ small onion, peeled
2 or 3 sprigs parsley
2 tablespoons butter, softened
½ teaspoon prepared mustard
8 slices white bread, toasted
8 slices Cheddar cheese

1. In the food processor or a blender, combine the deviled ham, onion, parsley, butter and mustard. Blend until the onion and parsley are finely chopped.
2. Spread the ham mixture on the toast slices.
3. Top each toast slice with a cheese slice.
4. Broil several inches from the heat for about 3 minutes or until the cheese starts to melt.
5. Cut the slices in half to serve.

Makes 16 snacks

Cheese Chutney Squares

Add a bright touch to an appetizer tray with these simple little canapés. You can prepare Cheese Chutney Squares at a moment's notice when you use the shredding blade of the food processor or multipurpose machine to shred the cheese.

5 slices sandwich bread, toasted
Softened butter
3 ounces Cheddar cheese, chilled
2 tablespoons chutney
½ teaspoon Worcestershire sauce
1 egg white
Cherry tomato wedges
Parsley sprigs

1. Butter the toast and trim off the crusts. Cut each slice into 4 squares and arrange them on a baking sheet.
2. Shred the cheese and chutney.
3. Stir the cheese, chutney and Worcestershire sauce together.
4. Beat the egg white with a whisk or beater just until it holds soft peaks.
5. Fold the cheese into the egg whites.
6. Spoon the cheese mixture onto the bread squares.
7. Broil about 5 to 6 inches from the heat just until puffy and browned.
8. Garnish with the cherry tomato wedges and parsley.

Makes 20 squares

Cheese Wafers

These very tender, cookie-like morsels are delightful with a glass of wine, with fruit, along with a main-dish salad, or for just plain snacking. Watch out, though — it is hard to stop nibbling them! A shredding blade will quickly shred the cheese. The food processor's steel blade or a blender container handle the rest of the recipe.

8 ounces sharp Cheddar or aged Swiss cheese, chilled
3 cups all-purpose flour
1 teaspoon salt
1 cup butter
4 ounces walnuts

1. Shred the cheese; set it aside.
2. Put the flour, salt and butter in the food processor (steel blade) or in a blender container. Blend until crumbly.
3. Add the nuts and cheese to the flour-butter mixture and mix just until nuts are coarsely chopped.
4. Turn the dough out onto waxed paper and push it into a ball.
5. Divide the dough in half and form each into a roll about 2 inches in diameter.
6. Wrap the rolls in protective wrap and chill for several hours.
7. Slice each wafer ⅛ inch thick and arrange them on lightly-greased baking sheets.
8. Bake the wafers in a preheated 350°F oven about 10 to 12 minutes or until lightly browned.

Makes 4 to 5 dozen wafers

Variations: Add any one of the following to the dough at step 2: 1 teaspoon caraway seed; ½ teaspoon dried dill weed or seed; 1 to 2 teaspoons poppy seed.

Appetizers

Celebration Cheese Ball

This nippy concoction will add zest to party fare. It is quick and easy to prepare in advance with the steel blade of the food processor or the shredding blade and blender of a multipurpose machine.

1 cup loosely-packed parsley
    sprigs
4 ounces sharp Cheddar cheese,
    chilled
4 ounces Swiss cheese, chilled
1 package (3 ounces) cream
    cheese, cubed
1 teaspoon Worcestershire sauce
½ teaspoon paprika
¼ teaspoon garlic powder

1. Chop the parsley in the food processor or blender container. Set it aside.
2. Finely shred the Cheddar and Swiss cheeses in the processor or with shredding blade of a multipurpose machine.
3. Combine with the cream cheese, Worcestershire sauce, paprika and garlic powder in the food processor or blender container. Blend until smooth.
4. Shape the cheese mixture into a ball.
5. Roll the ball in the reserved, chopped parsley.
6. Wrap tightly in protective wrap.
7. Chill thoroughly before serving with party rye slices, crackers or toast rounds.

Makes 1 ball, 3 to 3½ inches in diameter

Curried Cheese Dip

Traditional curry condiments give this dip an exotic flavor. It is tasty with fresh fruit — and a delight to prepare with a shredding blade and either the steel blade of the food processor or the blender of a multipurpose machine.

1 to 1½ ounces fresh coconut, cut
    in 1-inch pieces, or ½ cup
    flaked coconut
1 package (8 ounces) cream
    cheese, cubed
3 tablespoons raisins or currants
2 tablespoons salted peanuts
2 tablespoons milk
¼ to ½ teaspoon curry powder
    Fresh fruit

1. Shred the coconut with the shredding blade. Toast by spreading on a baking sheet and baking in a 375°F oven just until golden. Set it aside.
2. Put the cream cheese, raisins, peanuts, milk and curry powder in the food processor or blender container. Turn the motor on and off quickly just until raisins and nuts are chopped and mixture is combined.
3. Stir in the reserved coconut. Cover the dip and chill to blend the flavors.
4. If necessary, before serving stir in additional milk, 1 tablespoon at a time, until it is of dipping consistency.
5. Serve the dip with apple or pear wedges, banana chunks or other fresh fruits.

Makes about 1¼ cups

Crab Quiche Tarts

Here is a sneaky, quick way to make flaky tart shells with a convenience mix. A plastic food processor blade or multipurpose machine's mixer make quick work of combining the pat-in-pan dough. The savory filling is hard to beat but easy to mix using a shredding blade and the steel blade of a food processor or blender container. The directions are for muffin cups 2½ inches in diameter, but you can use the ingredient amounts in parentheses if your muffin pans have cups 2¾ inches in diameter.

Tart Shells
1 package (11 ounces) pie crust
    mix
3 tablespoons water
1 egg

Filling
4 ounces Swiss cheese, chilled
1 package (6 ounces) frozen
    crabmeat, thawed, drained
    and coarsely flaked
6 eggs
1 cup mayonnaise
¾ cup light cream or half and half
2 green onions, cut into short
    lengths
½ teaspoon dry mustard
¼ teaspoon salt
    Dash pepper

1. Place the pie crust mix, water and egg in the food processor or mixer.
2. Turn the processor on and off quickly or beat with the mixer just until the dough forms a ball on the beaters.
3. Using 2 (3) rounded teaspoons of dough for each tart, press the dough onto the bottom and sides of 24 (16) muffin cups that are 2½ (2¾) inches in diameter.
4. Shred the cheese with a shredding blade and sprinkle 2 (3) teaspoons into each tart shell.
5. Place the remaining ingredients in the food processor (steel blade) or blender container and blend just until the onion is chopped.
6. Spoon about 2 (3) tablespoons of the mixture into each tart shell over the cheese and crab.
7. Bake the tarts in a preheated 400°F oven 25 to 30 (30 to 35) minutes, or until puffed and brown and a knife inserted near the center comes out clean.
8. Cool the tarts on a wire rack 5 minutes before serving. Refrigerate any leftovers to reheat or serve cold.

Makes 24 (16) tarts

Blue Cheese Beef Balls

An easy appetizer you can put together far in advance, this recipe combines three strong-tasting ingredients — smoked beef, blue cheese and horseradish — for a nippy treat that is delicious with salted nuts and cocktails.

1 package (5 ounces) smoked
    sliced beef
1 package (8 ounces) cream
    cheese, cubed
2 tablespoons blue cheese
¼ small onion, peeled
1 tablespoon prepared
    horseradish
4 sprigs parsley

1. Combine beef, cream cheese, blue cheese, onion and horseradish in processor or blender and blend until onion is finely chopped.
2. Turn out into a small bowl and chill.
3. Chop parsley in processor or blender.
4. Form chilled cheese mixture into balls about ¾ inch in diameter.
5. Roll balls in chopped parsley. Cover and chill.

Makes 2 dozen balls

Cheese Wine Dip

The hint of wine makes this dip a perfect mate for sliced apples or sliced fresh fruits. The whole recipe is made in the food processor with its steel blade or in the blender container of a multipurpose machine.

1 small onion, peeled and
    quartered
1 package (7 ounces) Edam
    cheese
2 packages (3 ounces each)
    cream cheese
¼ cup port wine or sherry or
    apple cider
¼ cup light cream or half and
    half
¼ teaspoon celery salt

1. Chop the onion in the food processor or blender container.
2. Cut the Edam cheese into chunks. Add it to the processor or blender.
3. Add all the remaining ingredients. Blend until smooth.

Makes about 2 cups

Tuna Pâté

For instant hospitality, mix up this pâté and serve it as a dip with raw zucchini slices or wheat wafers. For a formal appetizer, chill the pâté in a mold and decorate it with radish slices and black olives.

1 package (8 ounces) cream
    cheese
1 can (7 ounces) tuna, drained
½ cup mayonnaise
6 large pitted ripe olives
2 scallions or green onions, cut in
    short lengths
2 tablespoons lemon juice
2 or 3 sprigs parsley
¼ teaspoon salt
    Dash hot pepper sauce

1. Blend all the ingredients until smooth.
2. Pour them into a bowl and serve as a dip or chill to serve as a spread.
3. To mold the pâté, pour it from the processor or blender container into a 2 cup mold or small bowl lined with plastic wrap. Chill thoroughly, then unmold and peel off the wrap to serve.

Makes about 2 cups

Quick Appetizer Ideas

Dips are still a mainstay on many an appetizer or cocktail table. Try one of the following, mixing it quickly and easily in the food processor or blender of a multipurpose machine.

Polynesian Dip: 8 ounces cream cheese, ⅓ cup dairy sour cream, 2 to 3 pieces crystallized ginger, ½ cup drained water chestnuts and 2 green onions, cut in short lengths. Blend until the ginger, chestnuts and onions are finely chopped. Add 1 teaspoon curry powder, if you wish. Makes about 2 cups.

Saucy Frankfurters: Cocktail franks are easy to make with the slicing blade of the food processor or multipurpose machine. Use 1 package (1 pound) of regular-sized franks. Fill the feed tube with franks and slice them with the slicing blade. Heat 1 jar (10 ounces) currant jelly in a saucepan or chafing dish with ⅓ cup prepared mustard. Add the frank slices and heat them through to make about 12 appetizer servings.

Cheese Stuffed Mushrooms

Stuffed mushrooms always make an elegant and satisfying appetizer and these are especially good and exceptionally easy — particularly when you use the shredding blade of a multipurpose machine or food processor to shred the cheese.

20 large fresh mushrooms, about
     1½ inches in diameter
   Lemon juice
   Salt
 4 ounces Cheddar cheese,
     chilled
⅓ cup herb-seasoned croutons
 4 slices bacon, crisp-cooked,
     drained and crumbled

1. Gently twist the stems and pull them from the mushrooms. Reserve the stems to chop for other uses.
2. Sprinkle the mushroom caps with lemon juice and salt and arrange them on a greased baking sheet.
3. Shred the cheese and croutons. Stir to mix.
4. Spoon the cheese-crouton mixture into the mushroom caps.
5. Sprinkle the crumbled bacon over the filled mushrooms.
6. Bake them in a preheated 400°F oven about 10 minutes. Serve hot.

Makes 20 mushrooms

Cajun Shrimp Balls

Form the shrimp mixture into tiny balls just big enough for one savory bite — your guests will find them irresistible. You can easily double the recipe for a group of more than 6 or 8.

3 green onions and tops, cut in
     short lengths
6 to 8 sprigs parsley
2 tablespoons butter
2 tablespoons flour
½ cup milk
½ teaspoon salt
¼ teaspoon hot pepper sauce
½ pound cooked shrimp
2 eggs
4 slices very dry toast

1. Chop the onions and parsley in the food processor or blender container of a multipurpose machine.
2. Melt the butter in a saucepan.
3. Blend in the flour.
4. Add the milk, salt and pepper sauce; cook and stir over medium-high heat until smooth and thick. Remove the saucepan from the heat.
5. Chop shrimp finely in the food processor or blender container.
6. Stir the shrimp into the sauce mixture.
7. Shape the shrimp mixture into balls about ½ inch in diameter.
8. Beat the eggs, pour them into a shallow bowl or plate.
9. Make toast into bread crumbs in the food processor or blender container and turn the crumbs into another shallow bowl or plate.
10. Dip the shrimp balls in the crumbs, then in the beaten egg, then again in the crumbs.
11. Arrange the balls on a plate or pan, cover it loosely with plastic wrap and chill about 1 hour.
12. Heat 3 to 4 inches of oil in a deep saucepan or deep fryer to 350°F.
13. Add the shrimp balls, a few at a time, and fry 3 to 4 minutes or until golden brown.
14. Keep the cooked shrimp balls warm in a 250° oven while frying the remaining balls. Serve with appetizer picks.

Makes about 3½ to 4 dozen balls

Salmon Savory

This piquant mixture is magnificent on hot rounds of party rye. For the calorie-conscious, serve it well-chilled on lettuce leaves with raw vegetable pieces. It is quickly prepared with the steel blade of the food processor or blender of a multipurpose machine.

1 can (16 ounces) salmon, drained
1 cup dairy sour cream
1 green onion, cut in short lengths
2 tablespoons lemon juice
½ teaspoon dried dill weed
½ teaspoon salt
1 loaf (8 ounces) party rye slices,
     or lettuce leaves and raw
     vegetable pieces

1. Combine the salmon, sour cream, onion, lemon juice, dill weed and salt in the food processor or blender container.
2 Turn the motor on and off quickly just until onions are chopped and mixture is combined.
3. To serve hot: Place about 1 tablespoon of the mixture on each bread slice. Place the slices on an ungreased baking sheet. Bake in a preheated 400°F oven 10 to 15 minutes.
4. To serve cold: Cover the salmon and chill several hours to blend the flavors. Serve it on a bed of lettuce with raw vegetables.

Makes about 32 hot appetizers
or 2¼ cups cold dip

Potato Cookies

These surprise nibbles may steal the show at a cocktail party. They are crisp and flavored with Parmesan cheese — perfect with before dinner drinks. Use the shredding blade of the processor or multipurpose machine for the potato and onion. You can mix the dough in the food processor or with the mixer of a multipurpose machine.

1 medium potato, cooked and peeled
½ medium onion, peeled and quartered
¼ cup butter, softened
1 cup flour
¼ cup grated Parmesan cheese
½ teaspoon baking powder
½ teaspoon celery salt
Grated Parmesan cheese

1. Shred the potato and onion.
2. Mix the vegetables with butter, then add the flour, Parmesan cheese, baking powder and celery salt. Mix until blended.
3. Pinch off pieces of the dough and form them into balls ½ inch in diameter.
4. Arrange the balls several inches apart on a greased baking sheet.
5. Press the balls flat with the bottom of a glass dipped in grated Parmesan cheese.
6. Bake the cookies in a preheated 375°F oven 20 to 25 minutes, or until browned and crisp.
7. Place them on a wire rack. Serve the cookies warm or cooled.

Makes about 3 dozen cookies

Triple Cheese Dunk

Cream cheese is the base for a pair of stronger-flavored cheeses in this dip. The recipe calls for Cheddar and Parmesan along with the cream cheese, but you could try Swiss and Parmesan, Muenster and Swiss, or Edam and Muenster. Triple Cheese Dunk is also great as a spread for ham sandwiches. Use the steel blade of the food processor or mix the dip in the blender container of another machine.

1 package (8 ounces) cream cheese, softened
6 ounces sharp Cheddar cheese
¼ cup grated Parmesan cheese
3 tablespoons milk
2 tablespoons mayonnaise
1 tablespoon lemon juice
1 teaspoon prepared horseradish
½ teaspoon seasoned salt

1. Combine all ingredients and blend until smooth. (You may want to shred the hard cheeses with a shredding blade first, then combine them with the rest of the ingredients.)
2. Serve with apple or pear slices, assorted wafers or chips.

Makes about 2½ cups dip

Cheddar Cheese Candle

Impressive as a buffet centerpiece or as a highlight on an appetizer tray, no one will guess how easy this candle is to make. A shredding blade quickly shreds the cheese. The nuts can be chopped in the food processor with its steel blade, or in the blender of a multipurpose machine.

10 ounces Cheddar cheese, chilled
2 tablespoons milk
1 cup pecans or walnuts
1 strip orange or lemon peel

1. Shred the cheese and set it aside to come to room temperature.
2. Beat the cheese and milk together with a mixer or wooden spoon.
3. Shape the cheese into a candle shape.
4. Finely chop the pecans in a blender or the food processor (use the steel blade).
5. Press the nuts around base of the cheese candle.
6. Chill until about 1 hour before serving, then let it come to room temperature.
7. Poke the piece of peel in the top to make the "flame." Spread the cheese on crackers to serve.

Makes 1½ cups, or 1 candle

Soups

A hearty, full-meal chowder
can have your family cheering
for more; a delicate melànge
of puréed vegetables and
cream can make your
reputation as a gourmet cook.

Iced Curry Seafood Soup

Gazpacho

A fire-and-ice refresher from Spain, Gazpacho has many variations. The quickest version of this classic salad-soup is made using the steel blade of the food processor or in the blender container of a multipurpose machine. You can control the amount of "fire" by varying the cayenne or adding hot pepper sauce. Prepare the soup far enough in advance for it to be icy-cold when served. For contrasting texture, a garnish of coarsely chopped vegetables and croutons is added before serving. Chill the ingredients ahead of time to shorten the refrigeration period.

Soup
- 2 medium tomatoes, peeled and quartered
- 1 onion, peeled and quartered
- 1 green pepper, quartered and seeded
- 1 cucumber, cut in chunks
- 2 cups tomato juice
- 1 tablespoon tarragon vinegar or wine vinegar
- ½ to 1 teaspoon salt
  Dash cayenne and/or hot pepper sauce

Garnish
- 1 cucumber, cut in chunks
- 1 green pepper, quartered and seeded
- 1 tomato
- 1 onion, peeled and quartered
- 1 stalk celery
- 2 tablespoons oil
- 1 clove garlic, crushed or minced
- 2 slices bread, cubed

Soup

1. Put the 2 tomatoes, 1 onion, 1 green pepper and 1 cucumber into the processor or blender container. Blend until smooth. Pour the soup into a container for refrigeration.

2. Add the tomato juice, vinegar and seasonings; stir to mix. Chill thoroughly.

Garnish

3. Before serving, coarsely chop the remaining cucumber, green pepper, tomato, onion and celery by putting one vegetable at a time into the processor or blender container and turning the machine on and off in short bursts.

4. Cover the chopped vegetables and chill them while preparing the croutons.

5. Heat the oil in a skillet; add the garlic and cook briefly.

6. Add the bread cubes. Cook and stir over medium-high heat until browned. Remove the croutons from the skillet and drain on paper towels.

7. To serve, ladle the smooth vegetable mixture into chilled bowls. Sprinkle with the chopped vegetables and top with croutons.

Makes 6 servings

Put the 2 tomatoes, 1 onion, 1 green pepper and 1 cucumber into the processor.

Blend until smooth, then pour the soup into a container for refrigeration.

Add the tomato juice to the soup in the container. To cut down on refrigeration time, have the tomato juice well chilled.

Stir the vinegar, salt and hot pepper into the blended vegetable mixture. Chill thoroughly.

Before serving, coarsely chop the remaining cucumber, green pepper, tomato, onion and celery for garnish. For big pieces, turn the processor on and off in short spurts and work with small amounts at a time. Cover and chill the chopped vegetables while preparing the croutons.

The bread should be cut into half-inch cubes. Firm white bread that is a day or two old makes the best croutons.

Heat the oil in a skillet; add the garlic and cook briefly. Then, add the bread cubes. Stir constantly over medium-high heat to brown them evenly. Drain them on paper towels.

Spoon the coarsely chopped vegetables onto the chilled puréed vegetable mixture. Serving in icers is an attractive way to keep the soup cold.

Scatter the crisp garlic croutons over the top of the soup for the final garnish and contrast of textures.

Gazpacho

Quick Vegetable Soup

When you do not have time to start a soup with a soup bone, you can create old-fashioned flavor by making this Quick Vegetable Soup — it calls for ground beef. You can grind the beef in the food processor with the steel blade or grinder attachment of a multipurpose machine. Then slice all vegetables with the food processor's or other machine's slicing blade.

1 pound ground beef
3 medium potatoes, peeled and cut in chunks
4 medium carrots, peeled and cut into short lengths
½ head cauliflower, separated into flowerets
2 medium onions, peeled
1 green pepper, seeded
1 medium zucchini or cucumber
4 cups water
2 beef bouillon cubes
2 cups or 1 can (16 ounces) tomato sauce
1½ to 2 teaspoons salt
1 teaspoon basil

1. Brown the beef in a large skillet or saucepan.
2. Slice the potatoes, carrots, cauliflower, onions, pepper and zucchini.
3. Add the vegetables to the beef along with the water, bouillon cubes, tomato sauce and seasonings.
4. Cover and simmer about 45 minutes or until the potatoes and carrots are tender.

Makes about 6 to 8 servings

Serving idea: Shred 4 ounces Cheddar cheese and sprinkle it over 6 to 8 pieces of toast. Float the cheese-toast on the soup in individual heat-proof bowls and run them under the broiler to melt the cheese.

Vegetable Soup with Liver Dumplings

This Vegetable Soup is savory and the Liver Dumplings are light and flavorful. This old-fashioned duo requires considerable slicing and chopping. Fortunately, the vegetables can be sliced with the slicing blade in the food processor or multipurpose machine; the livers can be chopped in the food processor (steel blade) or in a blender container.

3 carrots, peeled, cut in short lengths
3 stalks celery, cut in short lengths
2 onions, peeled and quartered
2 tomatoes
1 cup fresh shelled peas
2 quarts beef broth or stock
1½ teaspoons salt
1 clove garlic
1 teaspoon basil
1 bay leaf
Liver Dumplings

1. Slice the carrots, celery and onions with a slicing blade.
2. Peel and seed the tomatoes. Chop them coarsely with the steel blade of the food processor or in a blender.
3. Place the sliced vegetables, peas, beef broth and seasonings in a large saucepan.
4. Bring the soup to a boil and then reduce the heat and simmer it 15 minutes or until the vegetables are crisp-tender.
5. Drop in the Liver Dumplings. Cover and simmer 10 minutes.

Makes 8 to 10 servings

Liver Dumplings

2 slices bread
3 tablespoons cognac or water
1 pound chicken livers
2 eggs, separated
¼ cup butter
1 small onion, peeled
3 sprigs parsley
2 teaspoons salt
½ teaspoon pepper
2 tablespoons flour

1. Soak the bread in the cognac.
2. Chop the livers in the food processor (steel blade) or in a blender.
3. Add the bread, egg yolks, butter, onion, parsley, salt, pepper and flour. Blend until smooth, stopping the motor to scrape down the sides with a rubber spatula, if necessary.
4. Beat the egg whites with a mixer or rotary beater until stiff.
5. Fold the liver mixture into the egg whites and blend lightly.
6. Form the dumplings into egg shapes or round balls by pressing the mixture between 2 spoons; use the top of one spoon to push the dumpling into the simmering soup.

Makes about 15 dumplings

Soups

Mushroom Fish Stew

An astonishingly good fish and vegetable combination! Another surprise is the calorie cost — only 208 per serving. Use the processor's steel blade for chopping and slicing blade for slicing — or use the blender and slicing blade of a multipurpose machine.

1 medium onion, peeled and quartered
1 clove garlic
2 teaspoons oil
1 can (1 pound 12 ounces) tomatoes
1 bottle (12 ounces) clam juice
1 teaspoon salt
1 teaspoon oregano
¼ teaspoon pepper
1 pound fresh mushrooms
1½ pounds fresh/frozen halibut or cod steak
1 can (10 ounces) baby clams, undrained
2 or 3 sprigs parsley

1. Chop the onion and garlic medium-fine in the food processor or blender.
2. Heat the oil in a large saucepan or Dutch oven.
3. Add the onion and garlic and sauté about 2 minutes.
4. Add the tomatoes, clam juice and seasonings. Break the tomatoes into chunks with a spoon.
5. Heat to boiling, then reduce the heat, cover and simmer ½ hour.
6. Meanwhile, rinse the mushrooms and cut off the tips of the stems. Slice.
7. Cut the fish in 1-inch chunks by hand, discarding the bones.
8. Add the mushrooms, fish and clams to the pan. Cover and simmer 10 minutes longer.
9. Chop the parsley in the processor or blender and sprinkle it over the stew before serving.

Makes 6 servings

Iced Seafood Curry Soup

One sip and you will fall in love with this sophisticated soup — it is a superb balance of exotic spices and rich texture. The blender of a multipurpose machine or the food processor's steel blade handles the vegetable chopping. Since the whipping cream does not have to be whipped to stiff peaks, you can use the plastic blade in the food processor — or a wire whisk or electric mixer.

1 onion, peeled and quartered
1 celery stalk, cut in short lengths
1 apple, peeled, cored and quartered
½ carrot, cut in short lengths
¼ cup butter
3 tablespoons flour
1 teaspoon curry powder
½ teaspoon mace
2 cups chicken broth
2 cups whipping cream, divided
½ teaspoon salt
⅛ teaspoon cayenne pepper
1 bay leaf
8 ounces cooked crabmeat
8 ounces cooked shrimp

1. Chop the onion, celery, apple and carrot medium fine, using the steel blade in the food processor or a blender. Set them aside.
2. Melt the butter in a skillet and stir in the flour, curry powder and mace. Cook and stir over medium heat for 2 minutes.
3. Gradually add the chicken broth and 1 cup of the cream. Cook and stir over medium heat until slightly thickened.
4. Add the onion mixture, salt, cayenne and bay leaf. Simmer 20 minutes, stirring occasionally.
5. Cool the soup to lukewarm. Remove the bay leaf.
6. Pour the mixture into the food processor or blender and blend until smooth.
7. Strain the soup into a large bowl.
8. Whip the remaining cream until it is slightly thick. Fold the whipped cream into the soup.
9. Chill the soup for at least 5 hours or overnight.
10. To serve, stir in the crabmeat and shrimp.

Makes 6 to 8 servings

Quick Soup Ideas

Basic Recipe for Cream Soups: Melt 2 tablespoons butter in a saucepan, add 2 tablespoons flour and cook and stir until bubbly. Add 1 cup of milk and salt and pepper to taste to make the soup base. Then make your own improvisations. You can chop an onion in the food processor or blender and sauté it in the butter before adding the flour, if you wish. Use the food processor or blender to purée almost any cooked vegetable you like — from asparagus to zucchini. Or, shred 4 ounces of cheese to stir in the soup base for instant cheese soup. Try mixing ½ cup of peanut butter into the soup base for an unusual, delicious soup. Makes 2 servings.

For simple Cabbage Soup, slice or shred some cabbage, then cook it in chicken stock or broth or beef bouillon until crisp-tender. Shred some cheese to sprinkle over the top just before serving.

Try this easy Avocado Soup: Blend 4 peeled and pitted avocados, 3 cups cold chicken broth, 1 tablespoon lemon juice and a dash of salt and pepper; blend until smooth in the food processor or blender. Stir in 2 cups cold light cream and chill thoroughly. Absolutely elegant! Makes about 8 servings.

Broccoli Tuna Chowder

Crisp-cooked broccoli is the star of this hearty dish. A touch of white wine gives it a sophisticated flavor. Use the processor's steel blade or the multipurpose machine's blender or slicing blade to simplify preparation.

1½ pounds fresh broccoli, trimmed and cut in small pieces or 2 packages (10 ounces each) frozen chopped broccoli
2 cans (13¾ ounces each) chicken broth
2 medium onions, peeled and quartered
¼ cup butter
¼ cup flour
¼ cup dry white wine
1 teaspoon salt
½ teaspoon white pepper
1 can (7 ounces) tuna, drained and flaked

1. Cook the broccoli with 1 can of the chicken broth until just tender. Set them aside.
2. Chop the onion in the food processor (steel blade) or blender.
3. Melt the butter in another saucepan. Add the onion and sauté over medium heat until tender.
4. Blend in the flour and cook and stir until bubbly.
5. Add the remaining can of chicken broth and cook and stir until the mixture comes to a boil and is smooth and thickened.
6. Stir in the white wine, seasonings, tuna and broccoli mixture.
7. Heat until piping hot.

Makes 6 to 8 servings

Asparagus Soup

The extra tang of lemon peel and juice makes this soup taste just like asparagus with Hollandaise Sauce. The steel blade of the food processor or the blender of a multipurpose machine takes care of all the chopping and puréeing.

1 pound asparagus, washed and trimmed, cut in short lengths
2 cups chicken broth or stock
½ lemon
1 small onion, peeled
2 tablespoons butter
2 tablespoons flour
    Dash nutmeg

1. Cook the asparagus in the broth until tender, about 7 to 10 minutes.
2. Meanwhile, cut thin, outer portion of peel from the lemon with knife or vegetable peeler. Cut the white portion of peel and discard it. Quarter and seed the lemon and grate it in the food processor (steel blade) or blender along with the outer portion of the peel.
3. Add the onion to the lemon and chop finely.
4. Melt the butter in a saucepan. Add the onion-lemon mixture and sauté briefly.
5. Stir in the flour and cook until bubbly.
6. Pour the asparagus and broth into the food processor or blender container and blend until smooth.
7. Pour the puréed asparagus into the saucepan with the flour-lemon mixture. Cook and stir until it is smooth and thickened.
8. Sprinkle nutmeg over each serving.

Makes 6 servings

Cream of Cheese Soup

Serve this simple but satisfying soup to please the cheese-lovers in your family. They will clamor for more. Shredding is easy with the shredding blade of the food processor or multipurpose machine. Chill the cheese thoroughly for the best results. The food processor's steel blade or a blender can quickly chop the vegetables.

1 carrot, peeled and cut in short lengths
1 stalk celery, cut in short lengths
½ small onion, peeled
1 cup boiling water
½ teaspoon salt
¼ cup butter
⅓ cup all-purpose flour
2 cups milk
2 cups chicken broth
8 ounces sharp Cheddar cheese, chilled

1. Finely chop the carrot, celery and onion in the food processor (steel blade) or blender.
2. Cook the carrot, celery and onion in the boiling water with the salt until tender, about 5 minutes. Do not drain.
3. Melt the butter in a saucepan. Add the flour and cook and stir about 2 minutes. Add the milk and chicken broth; cook and stir until thickened.
4. Shred the cheese with a shredding blade.
5. Add the cheese to the saucepan and stir to blend. Add the vegetables and cooking water. Cook, stirring constantly over low heat until smooth.

Makes 6 to 8 servings

Brunswick Stew

An old-fashioned, long-simmered stock is the basis for this vegetable laden stew. Fortunately, the slicing blade of the food processor or multipurpose machine can prepare the vegetables quickly.

Stock

    4 to 5 pounds stewing chicken, cut up
    3 pounds ham shank
    3 to 4 cups water
    ½ cup celery leaves
    6 whole black peppercorns
    2 bay leaves
1½ teaspoon salt
    ½ teaspoon basil

Stew

    6 cups chicken and ham stock
    4 cups milk
    5 medium potatoes, peeled and cut in chunks
    3 stalks celery, cut in short lengths
    2 medium onions, peeled
    1 package (10 ounces) frozen Fordhook lima beans
    1 package (10 ounces) frozen whole kernel corn
    ½ cup all-purpose flour
    1 cup water
    5 cups cubed cooked chicken
    3 cups cubed or julienned ham
    2 tomatoes, peeled and cut in wedges

Stock

1. Combine all the stock ingredients in a large pot or kettle. Cover and simmer about 2 to 2½ hours or until the chicken is tender.
2. Lift the chicken and ham from the stock and cool. Cube the chicken and cut ham in cubes or strips.
3. Strain stock. Chill and remove the fat.

Stew

4. Measure 6 cups of stock in a large pot or kettle and add the milk.
5. Slice the potatoes, celery and onions with a slicing blade and add them to the kettle along with the lima beans and corn.
6. Cover and simmer about 10 minutes or until vegetables are just tender.
7. Blend the flour and water until smooth. Add them to the stew and cook and stir until thickened.
8. Add the chicken, ham and tomatoes and heat until piping hot.

Makes 10 to 12 generous servings

Note: If you want to freeze Brunswick Stew, wait and add the tomatoes when reheating it.

Brunswick Stew

World's Greatest Seafood Chowder

Truly worthy of its name, this chowder is flavorful, hearty and satisfying — everything a chowder should be. There is lots of chopping, and you save time and effort by using the processor's steel blade or the blender of a multipurpose machine.

1½ cups enriched durum small-shell macaroni
1 medium onion, peeled and quartered
2 stalks celery, cut in short lengths
1 clove garlic
¼ cup butter
⅓ cup dry white wine
1 teaspoon chicken base
1 teaspoon salt
½ teaspoon each thyme, nutmeg and pepper
1 bay leaf
5 tablespoons flour
⅓ cup cold water
1 pound codfish fillets (fresh or frozen and thawed), cubed
6 oysters or 1 can (10 ounces) frozen oysters, drained, reserve liquid
½ medium green pepper, seeded
1 can (8 ounces) evaporated milk
1 can (8 ounces) minced clams, drained, reserve liquid
1 can (4 ounces) tiny shrimp, drained, reserve liquid
2 or 3 sprigs parsley
1 jar (2 ounces) pimiento, drained

1. Cook the shells in boiling salted water (2 quarts water plus 1 tablespoon salt) until tender, about 8 minutes. Drain.
2. Chop the onion, celery and garlic medium fine in the food processor (steel blade) or blender.
3. Melt the butter in a large saucepan. Add chopped vegetables and sauté 5 minutes.
4. Combine the reserved liquid from the clams, shrimp and oysters and add enough water to measure 3 cups. Add the liquid to the sautéed mixture.
5. Stir in the wine, chicken base and seasonings. Cover and simmer 15 minutes.
6. Blend the flour and cold water to a smooth paste. Add it to the liquid in the pan, stirring constantly. Cook and stir until smooth and thickened.
7. Add the codfish and oysters.
8. Chop the green pepper medium fine, add it to the pan. Simmer uncovered 10 to 15 minutes.
9. Remove the bay leaf, then stir in the macaroni shells, milk, clams and shrimp.
10. Chop the parsley and add it to the chowder, then chop the pimiento and add it.
11. Heat to simmering and serve.

Makes 8 to 10 hearty servings

Chilled Avocado Soup

Sometimes known as "green gold," avocados achieve the height of their opulence when served in a creamy chilled soup. Though made in batches, this recipe is quick to fix in a blender or food processor with its steel blade. Make the soup and chill it just an hour or two before serving as avocado darkens when exposed to air.

3 medium avocados, peeled, seeded and cubed
2 cups chicken broth, divided
2 cloves garlic, chopped
1 tablespoon lemon juice
½ teaspoon salt
Dash cayenne pepper
1 cup whipping cream, divided
1 medium tomato, quartered
1 lemon, ends removed

1. Place the avocados, a few cubes at a time, in the processor or blender. Blend until puréed. If necessary, occasionally turn the motor off and scrape down the sides of the container with a rubber spatula. Continue until all the avocados are puréed.
2. Add ½ cup of the broth, the garlic, lemon juice, salt and cayenne. Blend until smooth.
3. Slowly add the remaining broth while the motor is running. Blend until smooth.
4. Pour half the mixture into a medium-sized bowl.
5. To the remaining mixture in the processor or blender, slowly add ½ cup of the cream while the machine is running.
6. Pour the blended portion of the soup into a 1½-quart, airtight, storage container.
7. Return the mixture in the bowl to the processor or blender.
8. Add the remaining cream slowly while the machine is running. Blend until creamy.
9. Add the tomato to the processor or blender. Turn the motor on and off quickly just until the tomato is chopped.
10. Combine the mixture with the soup in the storage container.
11. Seal and chill.
12. Just before serving, thinly slice the lemon with the slicing blade of the processor or multipurpose machine. Garnish the soup with the lemon slices.

Makes 8 servings

Pea and Provolone Soup

Pea and Provolone Soup

For a quick lunch, serve this tasty soup along with bread sticks or crusty French bread, a tomato salad and some fresh fruit. The shredding blade in the food processor or multipurpose machine make an easy soup even easier.

1 can (10 ½ ounces) condensed
    green pea soup
2½ cups milk
4 ounces Provolone cheese,
    chilled
2 frankfurters, sliced
    Provolone cheese (for garnish)

1. Heat the soup and milk to simmering.
2. Shred cheese with the shredding blade of the food processor or multipurpose machine and add it to the soup.
3. Stir over very low heat just until the cheese is melted.
4. Float frankfurter slices in the soup for garnish. Shred additional cheese for garnish, if desired.

Makes 4 to 6 servings

Oeufs Poché Potage (Poached Egg Soup)

This French recipe calls for a poached egg floating in each bowl of savory broth. Garlic can be added to suit your own taste. If you use a food processor you will need the slicing blade, steel blade and shredding blade. If you use a multipurpose machine you will need the slicing blade, blender and shredding blade.

1 medium onion, peeled and
    quartered
1 stalk celery, cut in short lengths
1 medium carrot, cut in short
    lengths
1 to 2 cloves garlic
2 tablespoons butter
4 cups beef broth
4 slices French bread, ½-inch
    thick, toasted and cubed
4 eggs
2 ounces Cheddar or Monterey
    Jack cheese

1. Slice the onion and celery with the slicing blade of the food processor or multipurpose machine. Set them aside.
2. Chop the carrot and garlic in the processor (steel blade) or blender by turning the motor on and off quickly.
3. Melt the butter in a large saucepan. Sauté the onion, celery, carrot and garlic in the butter for 2 to 3 minutes.
4. Add the beef broth to the saucepan. Bring it to a boil. Reduce the heat; cover and simmer 10 minutes.
5. While the broth simmers, place the toast cubes into 4 bowls.
6. Shred the cheese with the shredding blade. Set it aside.
7. Break the eggs, one at a time, into a shallow bowl. Hold the bowl close to the surface of the simmering broth and slip the eggs into the broth.
8. Simmer the eggs 3 to 5 minutes, depending on how well-poached you want them.
9. Transfer the eggs with a slotted spoon to the soup bowls.
10. Ladle the soup over the toast cubes and eggs. Sprinkle with the cheese.

Makes 4 hearty servings

Hearty Corn Chowder

The essence of a comfortable Sunday night supper, Hearty Corn Chowder is a delicious way to use leftover ham. The slicing blade on the food processor or multipurpose machine quickly handle the onions. The ham and potato can be chopped in the multipurpose machine's blender, or with the steel blade of the food processor.

2 onions, peeled and quartered 1 potato, peeled and cut in chunks ½ pound cooked ham 4 sprigs parsley 3 tablespoons butter 2 cups fresh corn kernels or 1 can (1 pound) whole kernel corn drained 1 can (10¾ ounces) condensed cream of mushroom soup 2½ cups milk 1 teaspoon salt ⅛ teaspoon pepper Butter	1. Slice the onions with the slicing blade of the food processor or multipurpose machine. 2. Coarsely chop the potato, using the food processor's steel blade or a blender. 3. Chop the ham and set it aside. 4. Chop the parsley. Set it aside. 5. Sauté the onions in the butter in a large saucepan until tender. 6. Add the potatoes, ham, corn, soup, milk, salt and pepper. Heat to boiling; reduce the heat and simmer until the potato is tender, about 20 minutes. 5. To serve, pour the chowder into bowls. Top each with a dot of butter and chopped parsley. *Makes 6 to 8 servings*

Vichyssoise Cresson

The classic potato-leek soup gets a new flavor and color with the addition of watercress — a beautiful, cool and satisfying soup. Let the steel blade of the food processor or the blender of a multipurpose machine handle all the chopping.

3 medium leeks or 6 to 8 green onions, washed and cut in short lengths ¼ cup butter 4 medium potatoes, peeled and cut in chunks 1 quart chicken stock 1 bunch watercress 1 teaspoon salt Dash white pepper 1 cup whipping cream Watercress (for garnish)	1. Chop the leeks in the food processor or blender. 2. Melt the butter in a large saucepan. Add the leeks and cook until they are limp, about 5 minutes. 3. Chop the potatoes in the food processor (steel blade) or blender by turning the motor on and off in short bursts. 4. Add the potatoes to the leeks along with stock. Cover and simmer about 15 minutes or until very tender. 5. Pour the potato mixture into the processor or blender and blend until very smooth. 6. Add the watercress and seasonings and blend until finely chopped. 7. Pour the mixture into a large container. 8. Stir in the cream. 9. Cover and chill thoroughly. Garnish with watercress. *Makes 8 servings*

Potage Pommes de Terre (Potato Soup)

Enriched with Swiss cheese, this robust potato soup is perfect to serve after skiing or any other outdoor activity. The shredding blade and the steel blade of the food processor or the blender of a multipurpose machine make the soup in short order.

4 medium potatoes, peeled and cut in chunks 4 ounces Swiss cheese, chilled 2 cups water 2 chicken bouillon cubes ½ teaspoon salt 1 small onion, peeled and quartered 2 tablespoons butter 2 tablespoons flour 2½ cups milk 2 or 3 sprigs parsley	1. Shred the potatoes with the shredding blade of the food processor or multipurpose machine. 2. Shred the cheese with the same shredding blade and set it aside. 3. Put the potatoes in a saucepan along with the water, bouillon and salt. Cover and simmer until tender, about 15 minutes. 4. Meanwhile, chop the onion in the food processor with the steel blade or in a blender. 5. Melt the butter in a saucepan. Add the onion and sauté until tender. 6. Blend in the flour and cook and stir until bubbly. 7. Add the milk and cook and stir until smooth and thickened. 8. Stir in the potato mixture and heat to boiling. Remove it from the heat. 9. Add the cheese to the potato mixture and stir until melted. 10. Chop the parsley with the food processor's steel blade or in a blender. Sprinkle it over the soup before serving. *Makes 6 to 8 servings*

Hale and Hearty Beef Chowder

Here is a full-meal soup that is easy enough to put together after work and impressive enough for an impromptu supper party. The shredding blade of any machine saves you hand-shredding the vegetables.

3 to 4 medium potatoes, peeled
   and quartered
1 small onion, peeled
1 stalk celery, cut into short
   lengths
¼ cup butter
1¼ cups water
1 tablespoon flour
3 cups milk
1 package (3 ounces) smoked
   sliced beef
1 teaspoon beef stock base
1 can (7 ounces) vacuum-packed
   whole kernel corn
1 teaspoon salt
   Dash pepper
1 cup dairy sour cream
2 or 3 sprigs parsley

1. Shred the potatoes, onion and celery with the shredding blade of the food processor or multipurpose machine.
2. Melt the butter in a large saucepan. Add the potatoes, onion, celery and water. Cover and simmer about 10 minutes or until the potatoes are tender.
3. Sprinkle the flour over the potatoes; stir in the flour and simmer another minute.
4. Gradually stir in the milk.
5. Tear the beef into small pieces and add them along with the beef stock base, corn, salt and pepper.
6. Blend in the sour cream and heat just until piping hot.
7. Chop the parsley in a blender or with the steel blade of the food processor and sprinkle over each serving as garnish.

Makes 8 to 10 servings

Hale and Hearty Beef Chowder

Chilled Mushroom Shrimp Bisque

A thick, rich shrimp soup, this bisque is delicious in summer or winter. Serve it with fruit salad and crisp bread sticks for a marvelous meal. The slicing blade of any machine can slice the mushrooms in an instant, then turn to the processor's steel blade or a blender container for the other chopping chores.

1 pound fresh mushrooms
1½ cups water
1 teaspoon salt
1 small onion, peeled
    and quartered
¼ cup butter
¼ cup all-purpose flour
1½ teaspoons salt
    Dash pepper
2½ cups milk
½ cup whipping cream
2 cups cooked shrimp

1. Rinse the mushrooms and cut off the tips of the stems. Slice with the slicing blade of the food processor or multipurpose machine.
2. Combine the sliced mushrooms, water and salt in a medium-sized saucepan. Cover and simmer 10 minutes. Drain, reserving the liquid, and set both the mushrooms and liquid aside.
3. Chop the onion medium-fine in the food processor or blender.
4. Melt the butter in a medium saucepan. Add the onion and sauté until tender.
5. Blend in the flour, salt and pepper and cook and stir until bubbly.
6. Add the mushroom liquid and milk and cook and stir until mixture comes to a boil and is smooth and thickened.
7. Remove the mushroom mixture from the heat and stir in the whipping cream.
8. Chop the shrimp coarsely in the food processor or blender.
9. Add the shrimp to the mushroom-cream mixture. Cover and chill thoroughly.

Makes 6 to 8 servings

Chilled Mushroom Shrimp Bisque

Soups

Waist Watcher's Cauliflower Soup

Robust and filling, this cauliflower soup is surprisingly low in calories. You can slice the cauliflower with the slicing blade of the food processor or multipurpose machine; shred the cheese with shredding blade of either machine. If you wish, purée the finished soup in the food processor or a blender container.

½ large head cauliflower,
    separated into flowerets
1 medium onion, peeled
3 cups water
3 vegetable bouillon cubes
½ teaspoon salt
½ cup nonfat dry milk powder
4 ounces Cheddar cheese, chilled

1. Slice the cauliflower and onion with the slicing blade of the food processor or multipurpose machine.
2. Combine the vegetables with the water, bouillon cubes and salt in a large saucepan.
3. Cover and simmer about 15 minutes or until cauliflower is tender.
4. Stir in the dry milk powder.
5. Shred the cheese and add it to the soup. Stir until cheese melts.

Makes about 8 servings

Spinach Soup Oriental

A savory, unusual broth, this would be an ideal accompaniment to an exotic, oriental meal. A blender or steel blade of a processor and a slicing blade are all you need to prepare it.

4 chicken breasts
4 cups water
½ pound fresh mushrooms
1 pound fresh spinach
2 green onions, cut in short
    lengths
¼ cup soy sauce

1. Cook the chicken in the water in a saucepan until tender.
2. Meanwhile, cut the ends of the stems off the mushrooms and slice them with the slicing blade. Set them aside.
3. Rinse the spinach in lukewarm water. Remove the stems and drain. Chop the spinach, a small amount at a time, in the food processor or blender container. Set it aside.
4. Reserving the broth, drain the chicken. Skin and bone it. Cut the chicken in 1-inch cubes. Chop the chicken with the onions, a small amount at a time, in the food processor or blender container.
5. Combine the chicken and onions, reserved mushrooms, spinach, reserved broth and soy sauce in a saucepan.
6. Bring the soup to a boil. Reduce the heat and simmer 5 minutes.

Makes 6 to 8 servings

Shrimp Creole Soup

The saffron adds a hint of exotic flavor to this piquant soup. Served with crusty French bread and a tossed green salad, it makes a charming light lunch. Always add gumbo filé at the end of the cooking time. The recipe can be quickly prepared in the food processor using the steel blade for chopping and the slicing blade, or using the blender and slicing blade of a multipurpose machine.

1 small onion, peeled and
    quartered
2 green onions, cut in short
    lengths
1 clove garlic
3 sprigs parsley
½ pound okra
1 bay leaf
3 tablespoons butter or oil
1 cup halved cherry tomatoes
4 cups beef broth or 3 cups beef
    broth and 1 cup clam juice
½ cup raw rice
⅓ cup dry white wine
1 teaspoon lemon juice
    Dash saffron
1 pound green shrimp
    Salt
    Pepper
    Gumbo filé

1. Separately chop the onion, green onions, garlic and parsley with the steel blade of the food processor or in a blender and set aside.
2. Cut the stems from the okra. Slice the okra with a slicing blade and set it aside.
3. Sauté the onion, garlic and bay leaf in the butter in a large saucepan until the onions are golden and tender.
4. Add the tomatoes, okra and parsley. Cook until the moisture has evaporated.
5. Add the beef broth, clam juice, cooked vegetable mixture, rice, wine, lemon juice and saffron. Bring it to a boil. Reduce the heat, cover and simmer until the rice is tender, about 20 minutes.
6. Add the shrimp to the soup. Cook until the shrimp turn pink, about 5 minutes. Salt and pepper to taste.
7. Ladle the soup into bowls. Sprinkle with gumbo filé.

Makes about 4 to 6 servings

Minestrone

Make the most of colorful, fresh vegetables by serving this Italian specialty as the main course. There is a lot less work to preparation when you let the slicing blade of the food processor or multipurpose machine slice the vegetables.

1 cup dried Navy beans
2 medium onions, peeled and quartered
2 tablespoons olive oil
4 medium carrots, peeled and cut into short lengths
2 medium potatoes, peeled and cut into chunks
1 small head cabbage, quartered and cut in wedges
2 stalks celery, cut in short lengths
2 medium zucchini
1 quart chicken broth, stock or bouillon
8 to 10 plum tomatoes or 1 can (1 pound) Italian-style tomatoes
½ to 1 teaspoon salt
1 cup rotini or any other pasta

1. Cover the beans with water in a large saucepan. Heat just to boiling, then remove the pan from the heat, cover and let it stand for 1 hour.
2. Meanwhile, slice the onions and sauté them in the oil until tender.
3. Slice the carrots and potatoes; set them aside. Slice the cabbage, celery and zucchini and set them aside in a separate bowl.
4. Add the chicken broth the beans along with the potatoes and carrots. Cover and simmer about 30 minutes or until the vegetables are almost tender.
5. Stir in the tomatoes, sautéed onions, cabbage, celery, zucchini, salt and pasta. Simmer uncovered 15 to 30 minutes or until the vegetables are tender.
Makes 8 to 10 generous servings

Minestrone

Salads

An attractively prepared salad is a joy to eat. Whether you like layers of crisp, fresh vegetables all uniformly sliced or prefer a spectacular molded salad, you will find a salad to suit your menu in this chapter.

Marinated Fresh Vegetables

Marinated Fresh Vegetables

Full of color, flavor and crunch, this wonderful salad can be made ahead of time. Leftovers keep beautifully, too. Use the slicing blade of the food processor or your multipurpose machine to prepare the vegetables. Remember, fill the feed tube of the processor gently but firmly and use the pusher to hold the vegetables in place as they are sliced — you will be rewarded with even slices as a result.

3 stalks celery
4 large carrots
3 green peppers, halved and
    seeded
3 small onions, peeled
3 tomatoes, halved lengthwise
    Basil French Dressing (see
    Dressings chapter)

1. Cut the celery into short lengths and slice. Empty the celery into a large bowl.
2. Cut the carrots into short lengths, about 3 inches long, cutting off the tips and stem ends. Slice and add them to the bowl with the celery.
3. Slice the green pepper halves. Layer them on top of the carrots and celery.
4. Slice and add the onions to the bowl.
5. Slice the tomatoes. Add them to the bowl.
6. Pour Basil French Dressing (see Dressings chapter) over the vegetables. Gently toss the salad to mix or leave the vegetables in layers.
7. Cover and refrigerate several hours or overnight.

Makes 8 to 10 servings

Thin slices, perfect every time, are easy if you learn just a few simple processor tricks.
Always trim off the ends of vegetables so a flat surface rests bottom down in the feed tube.
Also, if possible, select vegetables that will fit in the feed tube, such as small cucumbers and green peppers. Or, cut green peppers to fit in the tube. The feed tube should be packed as full as possible before slicing.

Cut the celery into 3-inch lengths and fill the feed tube full. Use medium-firm pressure on the pusher for even, thin slices. Cut the carrots in 3-inch lengths and pack them into the feed tube. Depending on the size of the carrots, you may have to halve any large ones lengthwise to fill the tube full. You will need to press down on the pusher firmly since carrots are hard.

If you are lucky, you may be able to find small peppers that will just fit into the feed tube. Otherwise, cut large peppers in half, seed them and fill the feed tube. A light pressure on the pusher is all you will need since peppers are delicate.

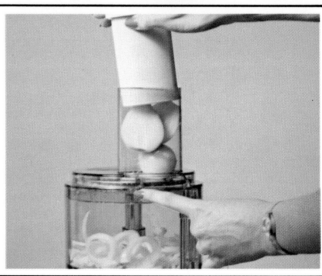

Cut the onions to fit the feed tube, if necessary. Pack them into the feed tube as firmly as possible and slice. Moderate to firm pressure on the pusher is important for even slices.

Stand halved or whole small tomatoes on end in the feed tube for slicing. Peel the tomatoes, if you wish. Just a little pressure is all you need on the pusher because tomatoes are soft. We suggest you use slightly firm tomatoes for slicing, rather than dead-ripe ones. Pour Basil French Dressing over the salad, then cover and refrigerate several hours or overnight.

Cucumber Mousse

Cool as its name, this molded salad makes a summer meal special or brings a touch of spring to winter menus. Made in the processor or a blender container, it could hardly be easier. On multipurpose machines you may wish to use the shredding blade for the cucumber and onion.

2 large cucumbers
1 small onion, peeled and quartered
1 lemon
1 lime
½ cup sugar
2 envelopes unflavored gelatin
1 teaspoon salt
   Dash cayenne
1 cup boiling water
2 stalks celery
4 sprigs parsley
1 cup whipping cream
   Thin lime slices (optional)

1. Peel and seed the cucumbers, cut them into short lengths and chop finely or shred along with the onion. Turn the vegetables into a bowl.
2. Cut several strips of the thin, outer colored portion of the peel from the lemon and lime. Put the strips in the processor or blender container along with the sugar, gelatin, salt and cayenne. Blend until the peel is grated.
3. Add the boiling water and blend until the sugar and gelatin dissolve.
4. Cut the white portion of the peel from the lemon and lime and discard. Cut the fruits into quarters. Add them to the processor blender container and blend until smooth.
5. Turn the gelatin mixture into the bowl with the cucumbers.
6. In a processor or blender container chop the celery and parsley until medium-fine.
7. Whip the cream with a mixer until stiff.
8. Add the whipped cream to the cucumber mixture along with the chopped celery and parsley and fold them together until blended.
9. Turn the mousse into a 5-cup mold. Chill it several hours or until firm.
10. Unmold the mousse onto a chilled plate and garnish it with thin lime slices.

Makes 6 to 8 servings

While you organize the ingredients for Cucumber Mousse, reflect on how tedious it would be to grate the cucumber, grate the lemon peel, squeeze the juice, and chop the onion all by hand.

Peel and seed the cucumbers and cut them into short lengths. Spoon or scoop out the seeds.

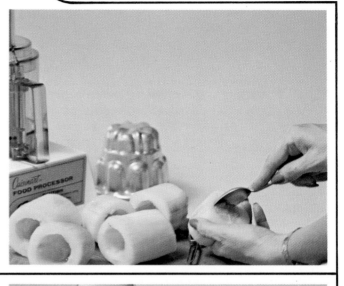

Using the steel blade of the processor, finely chop the cucumber and onion. Turn the vegetables out of the processor into a bowl.

Cut several strips from the thin, outer colored portion of the lemon and lime — use a sharp paring knife, vegetable peeler or twist cutter. Put the strips in the processor.

Add the sugar, gelatin and **seasonings** to the peel in the processor and blend until the peel is grated.

Add the boiling water and blend until the gelatin and sugar dissolve.

Cut the white portion of the peel from the lemon and lime and discard. Cut the fruits into quarters and add them to the gelatin mixture in the processor.

Combine the gelatin mixture with the cucumbers in the bowl. Chop the celery and parsley in the processor by turning the machine on and off in short bursts. Chop until they are medium-fine.

Whip the cream with a mixer or whisk until stiff. Add it to the cucumber along with the chopped parsley and celery.

Gently fold the ingredients together until blended, using a rubber spatula or whisk.

Turn the mousse into a 5-cup mold and chill for several hours or until firm. Unmold and garnish with thin lime slices.

Cucumber Mousse

Salads

Creamy Corned Beef Salad

The zesty cream base, spiked with horseradish and Dijon mustard, makes the perfect accompaniment for the corned beef. The steel blade of the food processor or the blender container of a multipurpose machine can handle all the ingredients' preparation.

1 package (3 ounces) lemon
  gelatin
1⅓ cups boiling water
1 cup mayonnaise
2 tablespoons prepared
  horseradish
2 tablespoons lemon juice
1 teaspoon Dijon mustard
4 stalks celery, cut in short lengths
½ green pepper, seeded
½ small onion, peeled
1 can (12 ounces) corned beef
2 hard-cooked eggs, sliced
  Crisp salad greens

1. Put the gelatin and boiling water in the food processor (steel blade) or blender. Blend until the gelatin dissolves.
2. Add the mayonnaise, horseradish, lemon juice and mustard; blend until smooth.
3. Pour the mixture into a shallow pan; chill in the freezer 15 to 20 minutes or until it begins to set around the edge.
4. Chop the celery, green pepper and onion in the food processor or blender. Place the vegetables in a bowl. Chop the corned beef coarsely. Add sliced eggs to the bowl.
5. Place the chilled gelatin mixture in the food processor or mixing bowl of a multipurpose machine. Whip until it is creamy and light.
6. Pour the gelatin mixture over the chopped vegetables and mix.
7. Pour the mixture into a 1½-quart mold. Chill at least 2 hours or until firm.
8. Unmold the salad onto crisp salad greens.

Makes 6 to 8 servings

Deli Cole Slaw

Deli Cole Slaw is crisp and colorful, flecked with red and green peppers and a shredded carrot. If you like long, thin strands of cabbage for your slaw, use a slicing blade; if smaller, juicier pieces are your choice, select a shredding blade. The food processor's steel blade or a multipurpose machine's blender can handle the chopping. Use your own homemade Mayonnaise to dress the slaw.

½ head (1 pound) cabbage, cut in
  wedges
1 medium carrot, cut in short
  lengths
1 small green pepper, seeded and
  halved
1 small red pepper, seeded and
  halved
½ small onion, peeled
3 sprigs parsley
1 cup Mayonnaise (see Dressing
  chapter)
2 tablespoons vinegar
2 tablespoons sugar (optional)
1 teaspoon seasoned salt

1. Slice or shred the cabbage. Set it aside in a large bowl.
2. Shred the carrot with a shredding blade.
3. Chop the green and red peppers, onion and parsley in the food processor (steel blade) or blender of a multipurpose machine. Add the vegetables to the cabbage.
4. Put the remaining ingredients in the blender or in the food processor (plastic blade) and blend until mixed.
5. Pour the dressing over the vegetables. Toss lightly to mix.
6. Chill until ready to serve.

Makes 6 to 8 servings

Quick Salad Ideas

For a crisp green salad that you can make ahead, use a slicing blade to slice some lettuce (about half a head), several stalks of celery, an onion, a green pepper and a can of water chestnuts (drained). Layer the vegetables in a pretty salad bowl. Shred 4 ounces of cheese and scatter it over the top, then spread the salad with 1¼ cups mayonnaise and sprinkle with some crisp-cooked and crumbled bacon. Cover and chill.

Super Slaws are easy as shredding cabbage in a food processor or multipurpose machine. For 6 to 8 servings, shred or slice half a head (1 pound) cabbage and then add the following dressing combinations: ¼ cup each mayonnaise and sour cream, ½ teaspoon dry mustard, 1 tablespoon chopped onion, 1 teaspoon salt, 1 tablespoon chopped pimiento.

A tasty slaw can be made without mayonnaise or sour cream. Shred half a head (1 pound) cabbage and then add 1 cup Basil French Dressing (see Dressings chapter), ½ cup chopped green pepper, ¼ cup chopped pimiento, and 2 tablespoons chopped parsley.

Carrot Raisin Salad is a great lunch treat. Shred several carrots, then mix them with ½ cup or so of raisins, ½ cup mayonnaise, perhaps a little salt and lemon peel, and then chill the salad until ready to enjoy. Makes 4 servings.

Moroccan Salad

Tangy spiced carrots and raisins make a distinctive salad. Try serving it with a lamb entrée or other dishes from the Middle East. The carrots can be sliced with the slicing blade of the food processor or multipurpose machine — a tiresome job by hand. The dressing can be prepared with the food processor's steel blade or in a blender.

1½ pounds carrots, cut in short lengths
4 cups water
1 cup red wine vinegar
8 whole cloves
4 cloves garlic, crushed
¾ cup raisins
Salt and pepper to taste

Moroccan Dressing
¾ cup cooled cooking liquid (from the carrots)
5 tablespoons olive oil
½ teaspoon cumin seeds

1. Slice the carrots with a slicing blade.
2. Combine the water, vinegar, cloves and garlic in a medium-sized saucepan.
3. Heat the seasoned water to a boil and add the carrots. Reduce the heat and simmer uncovered until the carrots are tender, about 20 minutes.
4. Remove the saucepan from the heat and use a slotted spoon to transfer the carrots, cloves and garlic to a large bowl. Reserve ¾ cup of the liquid for the Moroccan Dressing.
5. Toss the carrots, cloves, garlic and raisins with the salt and pepper.

Moroccan Dressing
6. Combine the reserved cooking liquid, olive oil and cumin seeds in the food processor (steel blade) or blender.
7. Blend 15 to 30 seconds and toss with the carrot-raisin mixture.
Makes 8 servings

Ruby Slaw

This rosy-hued combination is a delightful change of pace for a special outing. For coarsely-shredded cabbage, choose a slicing blade; for finely-shredded cabbage, use a shredding blade.

½ medium head red cabbage, cut lengthwise into small wedges
½ pound carrots, cut into short lengths
1 medium cucumber, pared, if desired
3 medium radishes, ends removed
Sweet and Sour Dressing (see Dressings chapter)

1. Shred the cabbage with the slicing or shredding blade, one or two wedges at a time. Empty the shredded cabbage into a salad bowl as necessary.
2. Shred the carrots with the shredding blade. Add them to the cabbage.
3. Slice the cucumber and the radishes with the slicing blade.
4. Toss the cabbage, carrots, cucumbers and radishes together with the dressing and serve immediately. Or, chill the vegetables, drain and toss them with the dressing just before serving.
Makes 6 servings

Fresh Tomato Aspic

Fresh tomatoes give this classic salad a zippy flavor that puts it a cut above the ordinary aspic. The tomatoes and vegetables can be chopped quickly with the steel blade of the food processor or in the blender of a multipurpose machine.

4 large tomatoes, halved and seeded
1 small onion, peeled, quartered
3 stalks celery, cut in short lengths
1 tablespoon sugar
1 teaspoon salt
1 bay leaf
2 envelopes unflavored gelatin
½ cup cold water
3 tablespoons vinegar
2 tablespoons lemon juice
½ teaspoon Worcestershire sauce
Crisp salad greens

1. Finely chop tomatoes, onion and celery.
2. Place the tomato mixture, sugar, salt and bay leaf in a medium-sized saucepan; simmer 30 minutes.
3. Sprinkle the gelatin over cold water in a large bowl.
4. Pour the hot tomato mixture over gelatin. Blend until the gelatin is dissolved. Add the vinegar, lemon juice and Worcestershire sauce. Remove the bay leaf.
5. Measure the mixture and add enough water to make 4 cups. Pour the aspic into a 4-cup mold.
6. Chill until firm. Unmold the salad onto crisp salad greens.
Makes 6 to 8 servings

Cardinal Salad Mold

A double-decker spectacular — this salad has an orange-lemon-flavored sour cream layer on top and a snappy beet and horseradish layer on the bottom. It is delicious served with cheese and cold cuts. The food processor (steel blade) or the blender of a multipurpose machine handle all the ingredients, from grating the citrus peel to chopping the celery.

Top Layer

1 package (3 ounces) orange-flavored gelatin
1 cup boiling water
¾ teaspoon salt
½ lemon
½ orange
1½ cups dairy sour cream

1. In a small bowl, dissolve the orange gelatin in the 1 cup boiling water along with the ¾ teaspoon salt. Chill until it begins to set.
2. Meanwhile, cut a thin, outer portion of peel from the orange and lemon halves with a knife or vegetable peeler. Cut off and discard the white portion of the peel. Seed the fruits and blend them with the peel in the processor or blender until finely grated.
3. In a mixing bowl, beat the thickened gelatin with an electric or rotary beater until fluffy, about 3 minutes.
4. Fold in the sour cream and orange-lemon mixture. Turn the mixture into a 6-cup mold and chill.

Bottom Layer

1 package (3 ounces) lemon-flavored gelatin
¾ cup boiling water
1 can (1 pound) diced beets
3 tablespoons cider vinegar
¼ small onion
2 teaspoons prepared horseradish
½ teaspoon salt
2 stalks celery, cut in short lengths

5. Dissolve the lemon gelatin in the ¾ cup boiling water.
6. Drain the beets, reserving the liquid. Add water to the reserved liquid to make ¾ cup, then add it to the lemon gelatin.
7. Blend the vinegar, onion and horseradish in the food processor or the blender until the onion is finely chopped. Add it to the lemon gelatin with the salt. Chill until it begins to set.
8. Coarsely chop the celery.
9. Stir the celery and beets into the lemon gelatin.
10. Pour the beet mixture over the sour cream layer in the mold.
11. Chill the salad until firm. Unmold onto a chilled plate.

Makes 8 to 10 servings

Cardinal Salad Mold

Hot Seafood Salad

Looking for a luncheon entrée? This rich, tangy, hot shrimp salad should fill the bill. The processor's steel blade or the blender container of a multipurpose machine chops the ingredients in no time.

8 ounces brick cheese, cubed
3 stalks celery, cut in short lengths
¼ green pepper, seeded
¼ small onion, peeled
1 pound frozen cooked shrimp, thawed
½ lemon
1 cup dairy sour cream
2 ounces blue cheese
1 teaspoon salt
¼ cup toasted slivered almonds
½ cup cornflake crumbs
2 tablespoons butter, melted

1. Coarsely chop the cheese in the food processor or blender. Set it aside.
2. Coarsely chop the celery, pepper and onion in the food processor or blender, turning the motor on and off in short bursts. Set them aside.
3. Coarsely chop the shrimp. Set them aside.
4. Cut the thin, outer colored portion of the peel from the lemon with a knife or vegetable peeler. Cut off and discard the white portion of the peel. Seed the lemon and put it in the processor along with the peel.
5. Add the sour cream and blend until the lemon peel is grated.
6. Add the blue cheese and salt and blend until the cheese is finely crumbled.
7. Combine the cheese, celery mixture, sour cream mixture, shrimp and almonds in a mixing bowl.
8. Spoon about 1 cup of the mixture into each of 6 buttered individual baking dishes.
9. Toss the crumbs and the butter and sprinkle over the shrimp mixture.
10. Bake the salad in a preheated 300°F oven 10 to 15 minutes or just until heated through.

Makes 6 servings

Hot Seafood Salad

Frosty Cheese Mold

Tart-sweet and creamy, this molded salad has the surprising accent of blue cheese — serve it with fresh fruits for a refreshing treat. The food processor (steel blade) or a multipurpose machine's blender can chop the nuts and beat the cheese to a velvet-smooth texture.

½ cup pecans
1½ cups cottage cheese
¼ cup blue cheese
1 envelope unflavored gelatin
¼ cup water
1 cup milk, divided
1 can (6 ounces) frozen limeade
   concentrate, thawed
½ cup whipping cream
  Salad greens

1. Chop the pecans in the food processor or in the blender container of a multipurpose machine; set them aside.
2. Blend the cottage and blue cheeses until smooth.
3. Sprinkle the gelatin over the water to soften in a small saucepan.
4. Add ½ cup of the milk and heat over low heat until gelatin dissolves.
5. Stir in the remaining milk along with the limeade, cottage cheese and blue cheese.
6. Whip the cream with a mixer or wire whisk until light and fluffy.
7. Fold the whipped cream into the cheese mixture along with the pecans.
8. Turn the salad into a 5-cup mold. Chill until firm.
9. Unmold the salad onto crisp salad greens.

Makes 6 servings

Frosty Cheese Mold

Molded Shrimp and Avocado Salad

Lemony and light, this pretty little salad makes a lovely luncheon feature or adds a special touch to a buffet. Let the processor's steel blade or a blender do all the work.

1 package (3 ounces) lemon-
   flavored gelatin
¼ teaspoon salt
1 cup boiling water
½ cup cold water
1 tablespoon lemon juice
½ cup mayonnaise
2 stalks celery, cut in short lengths
¼ small onion, peeled
1 medium avocado, peeled, pitted
   and cut in chunks
1 cup cooked shrimp
   Salad greens

1. Dissolve the gelatin and salt in the boiling water.
2. Add the cold water and lemon juice and blend.
3. Beat the gelatin mixture and mayonnaise in the food processor (steel blade) or blender until smooth.
4. Add the celery and onion and blend until finely chopped.
5. Add the avocado and shrimp and blend until coarsely chopped.
6. Turn the mixture into a 4-cup mold and chill until firm.
7. Unmold the salad onto crisp salad greens on a chilled plate.

Makes 4 servings

Tangy Potato Salad

You add the seasonings to the potatoes when they are still hot so they can absorb the tantalizing flavor of this version of potato salad. Choose a slicing blade to do the potatoes; then chop the other vegetables in the food processor (steel blade) or in the blender of a multipurpose machine.

4 medium potatoes, peeled
⅓ cup vinegar
1 tablespoon mustard seed
1 tablespoon celery seed
2 stalks celery, cut in short lengths
4 green onions, cut in short
   lengths
½ green pepper, seeded
4 hard-cooked eggs
¾ cup dairy sour cream
½ to 1 teaspoon seasoned salt

1. Slice the potatoes with a slicing blade.
2. Cook the potatoes in only enough water to cover for about 15 minutes or until just tender. Drain well.
3. Add the vinegar, mustard and celery seeds to the hot potatoes. Toss them gently to mix; cover and let them cool.
4. Chop the celery, onion and green pepper and add them to the potatoes.
5. Coarsely chop the eggs and add them to the potatoes along with the sour cream and salt.
6. Toss the salad gently but thoroughly to mix.
7. Cover and chill thoroughly.

Makes 6 servings

Tomatoes Continental

A main dish salad for an elegant, easy-on-the-waistline luncheon. The rainbow-colored filling can be prepared in advance with any machine's shredding blade for the carrots and either the steel blade of a processor or blender of a multipurpose machine for chopping the other vegetables.

¼ pound carrots, cut in short
   lengths
2 stalks celery, cut in short lengths
1 green onion, cut in short lengths
¼ cup mayonnaise or salad
   dressing
½ teaspoon seasoned salt
8 hard-cooked eggs, halved
6 large tomatoes
   Dried dill weed

1. Shred the carrots with a shredding blade. Set them aside.
2. Chop the celery in the food processor or blender. Set it aside.
3. Combine the green onion, mayonnaise and seasoned salt in the food processor or blender. Turn the motor on and off quickly, just until the onion is chopped.
4. Add the eggs to the food processor or blender. Turn the motor on and off quickly, just until the eggs are chopped.
5. Stir in the reserved carrots and celery.
6. Turn the mixture into a medium-sized bowl and cover.
7. Chill to blend the flavors.
8. Just before serving, slice the tomatoes in 6 sections almost to the stem ends.
9. Fill each with about ½ cup of the salad mixture. Sprinkle with dill weed.

Makes 6 servings

Waldorf Salad

Tart apples, crunchy nuts and celery make a winning combination in the traditional Waldorf Salad. With the slicing and chopping done in a wink, this favorite salad can appear on your menu more often. The apples can be sliced with a slicing blade of any machine. When chopping the nuts and celery, turn to the food processor's steel blade or the blender of a multipurpose machine.

3 tart apples, peeled
1 tablespoon lemon juice
1 cup pecans or walnuts
3 stalks celery, cut in short lengths
¼ cup mayonnaise
¼ cup dairy sour cream
2 teaspoons sugar
¼ cup raisins
   Crisp salad greens

1. Halve and core the apples. Slice the apples with a slicing blade. Transfer them to a bowl and toss with the lemon juice.
2. Chop the nuts using the steel blade of the food processor or a blender; add the nuts to the bowl with the apples. Chop the celery and add it to apples.
3. Stir together the mayonnaise, sour cream and sugar, then add them along with the raisins to the apple mixture.
4. Chill at least 1 hour to blend flavors.
5. If desired, serve the salad on crisp salad greens.

Makes 4 to 6 servings

Deviled Delight

Please every palate at your party with an assortment of the smoothest, fluffiest deviled eggs ever. Prepare these three unusual variations with a food processor's steel blade or the blender of a multipurpose machine.

Bacon Crunch Deviled Eggs
6 hard-cooked eggs
2 tablespoons mayonnaise or
   salad dressing
1 teaspoon Worcestershire sauce
¼ teaspoon celery seed
2 bacon slices, crisp-cooked,
   drained and crumbled

1. Cut the eggs in half lengthwise and remove the yolks.
2. Place the yolks, mayonnaise, Worcestershire sauce and celery seed in the food processor or blender container.
3. Blend until smooth, stopping the motor and scraping down sides of the container with a rubber spatula, if necessary.
4. Stir in the bacon.
5. Refill the egg whites using about 1 tablespoon yolk mixture in each egg white half.
6. Chill to blend the flavors.

Makes 12 deviled halves

Dilled Ham Deviled Eggs
6 hard-cooked eggs
3 tablespoons mayonnaise or
   salad dressing
¼ teaspoon dried dill weed
1½ ounces cubed cooked ham
   (about ¼ cup)

1. Cut eggs in half lengthwise and remove the yolks.
2. Place the yolks, mayonnaise and dill weed in the food processor or blender container. Blend until smooth, stopping the motor and scraping down sides of the container with a rubber spatula if necessary.
3. Add the ham. Turn the motor on and off quickly just until the ham is finely chopped.
4. Refill the egg whites using about 1 tablespoon yolk mixture in each egg white half.
5. Chill to blend the flavors.

Makes 12 deviled halves

Curried Tuna Deviled Eggs
6 hard-cooked eggs
3 tablespoons dairy sour cream or
   plain yogurt
¼ to ½ teaspoon curry powder
½ cup flaked, drained tuna

1. Cut the eggs in half lengthwise and remove the yolks.
2. Place the yolks, sour cream and curry powder in the food processor or blender container. Blend until smooth, stopping the motor and scraping down sides of the container with a rubber spatula, if necessary.
3. Stir in the tuna.
4. Refill the egg whites using about 1 tablespoon yolk mixture in each egg white half.
5. Chill to blend the flavors.

Makes 12 deviled halves

Sunshine Salad Mold

This American classic can be made in half the time when the carrots are shredded with the shredding blade of the food processor or multipurpose machine. The food processor (steel blade) or the blender of a multipurpose machine can be used to grate and liquidize the lemon peel and pulp.

2 lemons
½ cup water
2 envelopes unflavored gelatin
½ cup sugar
1 cup boiling water
1 can (8¾ ounces) crushed pineapple in pineapple juice
3 medium carrots, peeled and cut into short lengths
Salad greens

1. Cut several strips from the thin, outer colored portion of the lemon peel with a paring knife or vegetable peeler.
2. Grate the peel in the food processor or blender with the ½ cup water.
3. Cut the white portion of the peel from the lemons and discard it. Quarter and seed the lemons and blend them with the peel and water until smooth.
4. Stir together the gelatin and sugar in a small mixing bowl.
5. Add the boiling water and stir until the gelatin dissolves.
6. Stir in the lemon mixture and the pineapple with its juice. Chill.
7. Shred the carrots with the shredding blade of the food processor or multipurpose machine. Stir the carrots into the cooling gelatin mixture.
8. Turn the carrot-gelatin mixture into a 4- or 5-cup mold and chill until firm.
9. Unmold onto salad greens on a chilled plate.

Makes 4 to 6 servings

Crunchy Chef's Salad

Leftover roast or broiled meats come back for a second act disguised as part of a superb salad. The slicing blade of the food processor or multipurpose machine take care of the mushrooms in an instant. Most machines can also slice the cooked meat.

4 to 8 ounces cold cooked lean meat
¼ pound fresh mushrooms
¼ pound fresh spinach, washed and crisped
½ medium head lettuce
1 cup salted Virginia peanuts
Spice Trader Dressing (see Dressings Chapter)

1. Slice the meat and mushrooms with a slicing blade and put them in a large salad bowl.
2. Tear the spinach and lettuce into bite-sized pieces and add them to the bowl.
3. Sprinkle peanuts over the salad and toss lightly with Spice Trader Dressing.

Makes 4 large servings

Avocado Crab Mousse

Creamy avocado is mixed with crab for a suave mousse, ideal for a special luncheon. The blender container of a multipurpose machine or the food processor's steel blade chop and mix the entire recipe in seconds.

1 teaspoon unflavored gelatin
½ cup cold water, divided
1 package (3 ounces) lemon-flavored gelatin
1 cup boiling water
1 tablespoon lemon juice
¼ teaspoon salt
¼ teaspoon hot pepper sauce
1 avocado, peeled and seeded
1 stalk celery, cut in short lengths
¼ cup mayonnaise
¼ cup dairy sour cream
1 can (6½ or 7½ ounces) crabmeat, drained and flaked
6 pear halves, drained (canned or fresh), peeled and cored
Crisp salad greens

1. Sprinkle the unflavored gelatin over ¼ cup of the cold water to soften. Dissolve the lemon-flavored gelatin in boiling water in a large bowl. Add the unflavored gelatin and stir until dissolved. Add the remaining ¼ cup cold water, lemon juice, salt and hot pepper sauce; stir to blend. Chill until slightly thickened.
2. Place the avocado and celery in the food processor (steel blade) or blender and chop finely.
3. Add the mayonnaise and sour cream and blend until smooth.
4. Add the avocado mixture to the thickened gelatin mixture in the bowl.
5. Stir in the crabmeat.
6. Arrange the pear halves in an 8-inch square or 8-inch round pan. Pour the crab-avocado mixture on top. Chill at least 6 hours or overnight.
7. Cut into 6 sections to serve. Invert the salad onto crisp salad greens. If desired, serve with additional mayonnaise.

Makes 6 servings

Florida Fish Salad

Lots of crisp celery give a delicate flavor and delightful crunch to this light, orange-flavored salad. The slicing blade of the food processor or multipurpose machine can slice the celery and onion quickly.

8 stalks celery, cut into short lengths
1 red onion, peeled and quartered
½ cup mayonnaise
1 teaspoon salt
¼ teaspoon pepper
2 pounds filet of sole or flounder, cooked, chunked and chilled
1½ cups fresh orange sections
Tomatoes or radish roses

1. Slice the celery and onion with the slicing blade of the food processor or multipurpose machine.
2. Combine the celery and onion with the mayonnaise, salt and pepper in a medium bowl.
3. Add the fish and the orange sections and toss lightly to mix.
4. Serve the salad on lettuce leaves; garnish with tomatoes or radish roses.

Makes 8 servings

Elegant Pear Mold

This delicately flavored molded salad is pretty enough to star at any holiday meal, especially when made in a fancy mold. The steel blade of the food processor or multipurpose machine's blender can do the mixing.

1 can (1 pound) pear halves
1 package (3 ounces) lime-flavored gelatin
1 package (3 ounces) cream cheese, cubed
2 cups whipped topping or whipped cream

1. Drain the pears, reserving the syrup.
2. Add water to the syrup to make 1 cup. Put the syrup-water in a small saucepan and heat to boiling.
3. Remove the saucepan from the heat. Add the lime gelatin and stir until dissolved. Let it cool slightly.
4. Mix the gelatin and cream cheese in the food processor or blender until smooth.
5. Add the drained pears and mix only until coarsely chopped.
6. Pour the pear mixture into a medium-sized bowl and chill until it begins to set.
7. Gently fold in the whipped topping until blended.
8. Turn into 4 to 6 cup mold and chill until firm.
9. Unmold onto a chilled plate and serve with fresh fruits, if desired.

Makes 4 to 6 servings

Shrimp and Mushroom Salad

Sliced mushrooms marinate in a tart dressing for several hours to give a special zip to this impressive salad platter. The slicing blade of any machine can slice the vegetables; the dressing can be mixed with the food processor's plastic blade or in a blender.

1 pound fresh mushrooms
½ pound cooked shrimp
⅓ cup salad oil
3 tablespoons lemon juice
2 tablespoons white wine vinegar
Several sprigs fresh dill or basil or ½ teaspoon dried dill or basil
½ teaspoon salt
1 medium cucumber
6 radishes

1. Rinse the mushrooms and cut off bases of the stems. Slice and turn into a large bowl with the shrimp.
2. Blend the oil, lemon juice, vinegar, herbs and salt in the food processor or the blender container.
3. Pour the dressing over the mushrooms; cover and chill several hours.
4. Slice the cucumber and set aside.
5. Slice or chop the radishes.
6. Arrange the watercress around the edge of a large plate or 4 to 6 individual salad plates.
7. Ring outside of the plate with cucumber slices, then arrange the mushrooms and shrimp in the center.
8. Garnish with radishes.

Makes 4 to 6 servings

Florida Fish Salad

Elegant Pear Mold

Shrimp and Mushroom Salad

Dressings

Roquefort Cream Dressing

Basil French Dressing

Smooth and tangy, this simple dressing is delightful on vegetable salads, mixed greens, even citrus fruits or apples. Use the steel blade or plastic blade of the processor or mix the dressing in the blender container of other machines.

¼ cup tomato sauce
⅓ cup red wine vinegar
1 cup salad oil
1 tablespoon sugar
1 teaspoon salt
1 teaspoon basil
1 teaspoon Worcestershire sauce
¼ teaspoon dry mustard
¼ teaspoon pepper
⅛ teaspoon hot pepper sauce
1 clove garlic

1. Combine all the ingredients in a processor or blender container and blend until smooth and the garlic is minced.
2. Chill in a cruet or covered container until ready to use.

Makes about 1²/₃ cups dressing

Pour the tomato sauce and all the other ingredients into the processor container.

Process until smooth and the garlic is minced. Pour the dressing into a cruet or container with a cover for refrigerator storage.

Mayonnaise

For years regarded as the trickiest of cooking techniques, Mayonnaise is now virtually fail-proof when made in the processor or blender. Homemade Mayonnaise has a flavor that surpasses anything store-bought — perfect for sandwiches, fruit salads, tender spring salads, or as the base for other dressings.

1 cup salad oil
2 eggs
2 tablespoons lemon juice or vinegar
1 teaspoon sugar
1 teaspoon dry mustard
½ teaspoon salt
Dash cayenne

1. Pour ¼ cup of the oil into the processor (using the steel or plastic blade) or blender container and add the eggs, lemon juice, sugar, mustard, salt and cayenne.
2. Process for about 5 to 10 seconds or blend at high speed.
3. Remove the pusher from the feed tube or remove the blender top and add the remaining oil in a fine stream while the motor is running.
4. When all the oil is added and the Mayonnaise is thick and smooth, turn off the motor.
5. Transfer the Mayonnaise to a covered container for refrigeration storage.

Makes about 1½ cups dressing

Mayonnaise comes from only a few ingredients — oil, lemon juice and seasonings — with eggs to act as the emulsifier. Mayonnaise can form the base of many savory dressings.

Pour ¼ cup of the oil into the processor; use either the steel or plastic blade. Add the eggs, lemon juice or vinegar, sugar, mustard, salt and cayenne. Process for 5 to 10 seconds.

Remove the pusher from the feed tube. With the motor running, add the remaining oil in a constant, thin stream throught the feed tube. Process until all the oil is added and the Mayonnaise is thick and smooth.

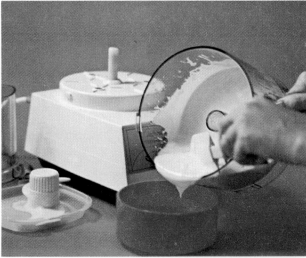

Transfer the Mayonnaise to a covered container for refrigerator storage.

Mayonnaise, Green Goddess and Thousand Island Dressings

Green Goddess Dressing

Transform your homemade Mayonnaise into a divine dressing. Parsley and green onions give it a delicate color while garlic and lemon juice add flavor and sour cream makes it extra rich. Green Goddess Dressing can be made with the steel blade of the processor or in the blender container of other machines.

1¼ cups Mayonnaise (see Mayonnaise recipe)
4 sprigs parsley
2 green onions, cut in short lengths
2 tablespoons lemon juice or tarragon vinegar or wine vinegar
½ clove garlic
½ teaspoon salt
Dash pepper
½ cup dairy sour cream

1. Prepare the Mayonnaise recipe and leave it in the processor or blender container.
2. Add the parsley, onions, lemon juice (or vinegar), garlic and seasonings; blend just until the onions are finely chopped.
3. Add the sour cream and blend just until mixed.
4. Transfer the dressing to a covered container for refrigerator storage.

Makes about 2¼ cups dressing

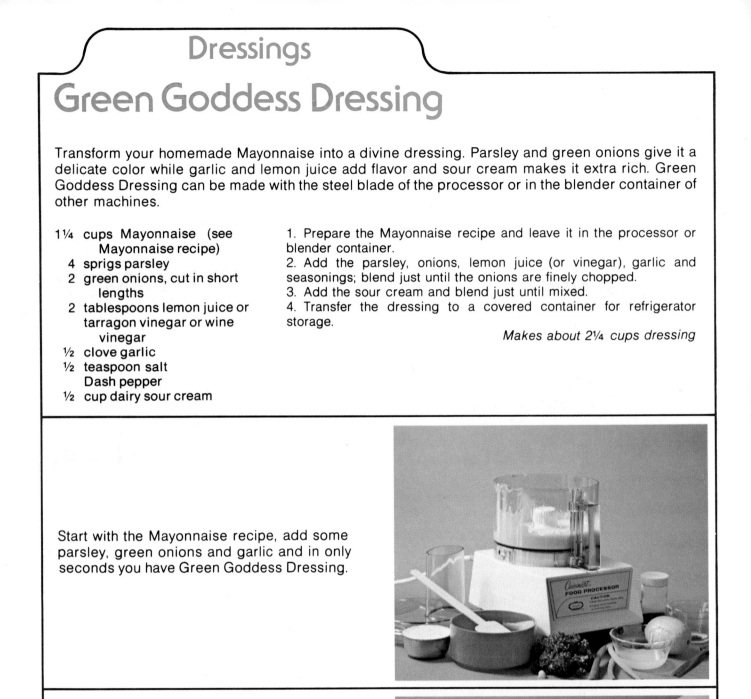

Start with the Mayonnaise recipe, add some parsley, green onions and garlic and in only seconds you have Green Goddess Dressing.

Add the parsley, onions, lemon juice and seasonings to the Mayonnaise in the processor. You can use tarragon or wine vinegar in place of the lemon juice.

Process just until the onions are finely chopped.

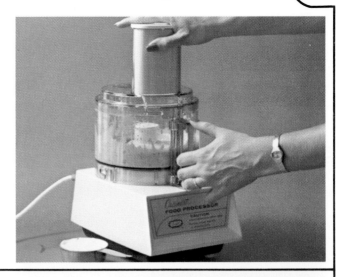

Add the sour cream to the mixture in the processor and blend just until combined.

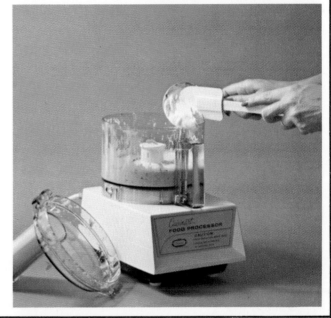

Transfer the Green Goddess Dressing to a covered container for refrigerator storage.

Thousand Island Dressing

Add chili sauce, seasonings, hard-cooked eggs and pimiento-stuffed green olives to your silky-smooth homemade Mayonnaise, chop them into a thousand pieces in a processor or blender and you have the perfect dressing for crisp hearts of lettuce — Thousand Island Dressing.

1¼ cups Mayonnaise (see
    Mayonnaise recipe)
¼ cup chili sauce
1 small onion, peeled and
    quartered
1 teaspoon salt
1 teaspoon paprika
    Dash pepper
2 hard-cooked eggs, quartered
8 pimiento-stuffed green olives

1. Prepare the Mayonnaise recipe and leave it in the processor or blender container.
2. Add the chili sauce, onion, salt, paprika and pepper. Blend briefly just to mix and to chop the onion.
3. Add the eggs and olives and mix until coarsely chopped.
4. Transfer the dressing to a covered container for regrigerator storage.

Makes about 2½ cups dressing

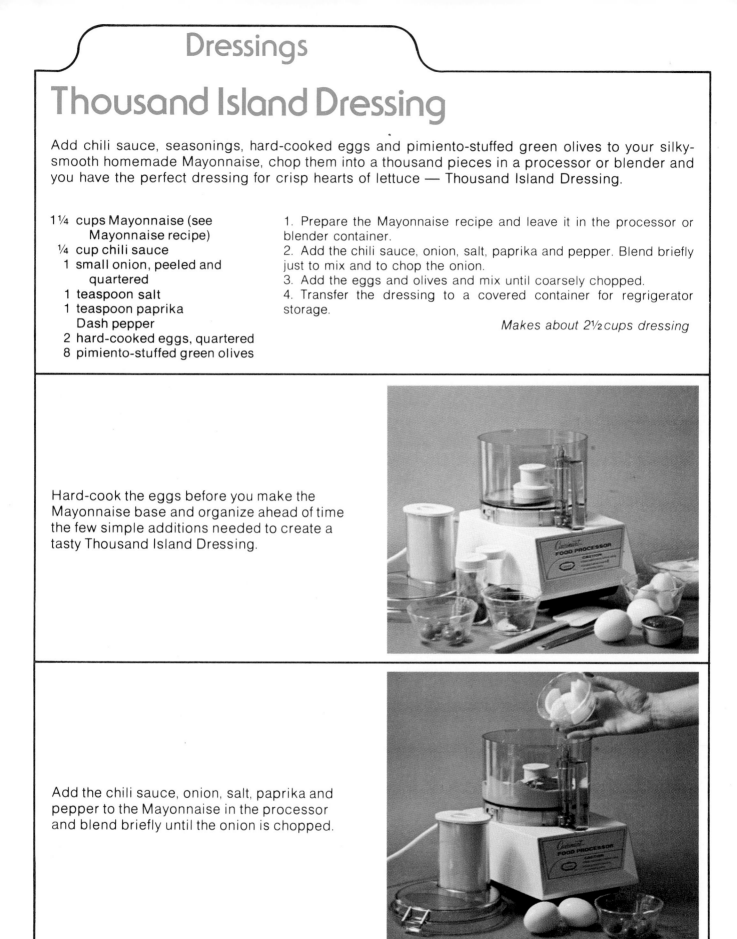

Hard-cook the eggs before you make the Mayonnaise base and organize ahead of time the few simple additions needed to create a tasty Thousand Island Dressing.

Add the chili sauce, onion, salt, paprika and pepper to the Mayonnaise in the processor and blend briefly until the onion is chopped.

Add the hard-cooked eggs and the olives. Turning the motor on and off in a few short bursts, coarsely chop the eggs and olives.

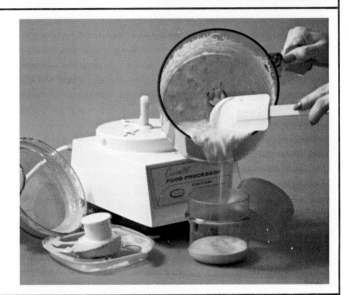

Transfer the dressing to a covered container for refrigerator storage.

Low Calorie Dressing

Everyone needs at least one low calorie dressing in his or her recipe repertoire. This one has a zip that will make you forget it has only about 20 calories per tablespoon. The steel blade of the food processor or a blender whips everything smooth.

¾ cup water
2 teaspoons cornstarch
½ onion, peeled
¼ cup vinegar
¼ cup catsup
2 tablespoons salad oil
1 teaspoon horseradish
1½ teaspoons sugar
1¼ teaspoons prepared mustard
½ teaspoon salt
½ teaspoon paprika
½ teaspoon Worcestershire sauce
1 clove garlic

1. Combine the water and cornstarch in a small saucepan. Cook and stir until clear and thickened, about 5 minutes. Let it cool.
2. Place all the ingredients in the food processor or blender and blend until the onion is chopped and the mixture is smooth.
3. Store in a covered container in the refrigerator. Shake well before using.

Makes 1⅓ cups

Roquefort Cream Dressing

Smooth, rich and superb — you may want to claim this as your own "House Dressing." It is made in a flash with the food processor's steel blade or a multipurpose machine's blender.

1 package (8 ounces) cream
    cheese, cubed
4 ounces Roquefort cheese
½ cup milk
2 green onions, cut in short
    lengths
2 sprigs parsley
2 tablespoons lemon juice
1 teaspoon salt
½ teaspoon tarragon
    Dash cayenne

1. Combine all ingredients in the food processor or blender.
2. Blend until smooth.

Makes about 2 cups

Spice Trader Dressing

An exotic dressing for tossed greens, vegetables, or meat salads, you have to make it several days in advance so the flavors have time to develop. The food processor's steel blade or a blender handle the whole recipe.

½ cup salad oil
3 tablespoons lemon juice
2 tablespoons vinegar
1 teaspoon sugar
1 teaspoon coriander seed
1 teaspoon cumin seed
1 clove garlic
½ teaspoon salt
    Dash cayenne

1. Combine all the ingredients in the food processor or blender.
2. Blend about 30 seconds or until well combined.

Makes about ¾ cup

Macaroon Dressing

Fresh fruit or pineapple salads deserve a special sweet dressing. This topping is so delicious you may be tempted to serve it as a dessert. Count on the food processor's steel blade or a multipurpose machine's blender to chop the macaroons and blend the other ingredients.

12 medium-sized soft coconut
    macaroons
2 cups dairy sour cream
½ cup packed light brown sugar
½ teaspoon vanilla extract

1. Coarsely chop the macaroons in the food processor or blender.
2. Add the remaining ingredients and blend just until mixed.
3. Allow the dressing to stand at least 6 hours to blend the flavors.

Makes 3 cups

Muy Picante Dressing

There is plenty of spunk in this easy-to-make dressing. Try it over sliced oranges or grapefruit, avocados or cold, cooked vegetables. All the mixing can be done in the food processor (steel blade) or a blender.

⅔ cup salad oil
¼ cup white wine vinegar
1 can (4 ounces) whole green
    chilies, drained
1½ teaspoons dry mustard
1½ teaspoons salt
1 teaspoon basil
    Dash white pepper
1 clove garlic

1. Combine all the ingredients in a blender or food processor.
2. Blend until the chilies are very finely chopped.
3. Let the dressing stand several hours to blend the flavors.

Makes about 1 cup

Sweet and Sour Dressing

Try this tangy delight on Ruby Slaw (see the Salads Chapter). It adds sparkle to fresh spinach salads, too. Whip it up in no time with the food processor's plastic blade or a multipurpose machine's blender.

¾ cup salad oil
⅓ cup sugar
3 tablespoons red wine tarragon
   vinegar
1½ teaspoons onion juice
¾ teaspoon salt
¼ teaspoon dry mustard

1. Combine all ingredients in a food processor or blender.
2. Blend until mixed.

Makes about 1 cup

Frozen Blue Cheese Dressing

Give fruit salads a gourmet treatment by topping them with cubes of this frozen dressing. The steel blade of the food processor or blender of a multipurpose machine chop the celery and do the mixing. For the fluffiest whipped cream, use a mixer, rotary beater or wire whisk.

1 cup whipping cream
3 stalks celery, cut in short lengths
1 package (3 ounces) cream
   cheese, cubed
⅓ cup Mayonnaise
1 tablespoon lemon juice
4 ounces blue cheese
½ teaspoon salt

1. Whip the cream until light and fluffy. Pour it into a bowl and set aside.
2. Chop the celery finely in the food processor or blender.
3. Add the cream cheese, mayonnaise, lemon juice, blue cheese and salt and blend until completely combined.
4. Add the whipped cream and blend just until smooth.
5. Spread the dressing in a shallow pan or ice cube tray. Freeze firm.
6. Cut the dressing in cubes to toss with a salad or serve on fruit.

Makes 4 to 6 servings

Frozen Blue Cheese Dressing

Main Dishes

Main dishes for all seasons and occasions are featured in this chapter. You will find stars for your formal dinners, as well as main dishes for light suppers, picnics and luncheons. Main dish attractions range from the elegant Orange Raisin Stuffed Lamb Roll to light meatless entrees such as Moule au Fromage (Molded Cheese Loaf).

Meat Loaf à la Roma

Swedish Meatballs

Finely ground meat and long beating make these tasty meatballs light and fluffy. Of course, "long beating" in the food processor or a multipurpose machine takes only a few minutes. The numbered directions in the recipe tell you how to make Swedish meatballs with a food processor. The photographed directions show you how to prepare the same luscious dish with a multipurpose machine like the Kenwood Chef.

3 slices firm white bread
1 cup light cream or half-and-half
1 medium onion, peeled and quartered
5 tablespoons butter, divided
¾ pound lean boneless beef, cubed
½ pound lean boneless pork, cubed
¼ pound lean boneless veal, cubed
1 egg
6 sprigs parsley
1 teaspoon salt
⅛ teaspoon pepper
⅛ teaspoon ground ginger
⅛ teaspoon nutmeg
2 tablespoons flour
¾ cup coffee
½ cup boiling water
1 beef bouillon cube

1. Tear the bread into several pieces and make bread crumbs in the processor container, using the steel blade. Turn the crumbs into a bowl.
2. Add the cream to the bread crumbs and let them stand while preparing the remaining ingredients.
3. Put the onion in the processor container and chop by turning the motor on and off in short bursts.
4. Melt 1 tablespoon of the butter in a skillet. Add the chopped onion and cook about 5 minutes or until tender.
5. Chop the beef in the processor until very fine. Place the beef in a bowl.
6. Chop the pork and veal together in the processor until very fine. Place them in a bowl.
7. Process half the beef and half the pork-veal mixture together for several seconds or until chopped very fine. Turn the processed mixture into the bowl with the crumbs. Repeat with the remaining meat.
8. Stir the meat mixture together with crumbs; stir in the cooked onion. Return the mixture to the processor container along with the egg, parsley and seasonings. Mix several seconds or until well blended.
9. Shape the meat mixture into 1½-inch balls, moistening your hands often with water to keep the meat from sticking.
10. Melt 2 tablespoons of the butter in a skillet. Add the meatballs as you form them and brown them on all sides over medium-high heat, turning often to keep them round. As the meatballs are browned, place them on a platter.
11. When all the meatballs are browned and are on the platter, add the last 2 tablespoons butter to the skillet and melt.
12. Stir in the flour and cook and stir until frothy.
13. Gradually add the coffee, boiling water and bouillon cube. Cook and stir until it is smooth and thickened, mashing the bouillon cube with the back of a spoon.
14. Return the meatballs to the skillet. Cover and simmer slowly for 25 to 30 minutes.

Makes 6 servings

To start making Swedish Meatballs, using a multipurpose machine like the Kenwood Chef, tear the firm white bread into sections and add them to the blender container. Blend to make crumbs. Pour the crumbs into the mixing bowl.

Add the cream to the crumbs in the mixing bowl and let them stand while preparing the remaining ingredients.

Quarter the onion and chop it in the blender container by turning the motor on and off in short bursts. Melt 1 tablespoon of the butter in a skillet. Add the onion to the butter in the skillet and cook until tender, about 5 minutes.

Grind the meats together in the grinder attachment twice. Add the egg and parsley to the meat during the second grinding.

Add the meat to the crumbs in the mixing bowl. Add the cooked onion and the seasonings to the meat in the mixing bowl.

Beat at medium speed until the meat mixture is very light and fluffy, about 5 minutes.

Melt 2 tablespoons of the butter in a skillet. Shape the meat mixture into 1½-inch balls, moistening your hands often with water to keep the meat from sticking. As you form the balls, add them to the skillet.

Brown the balls in the butter on medium-high heat, turning often to keep balls round.

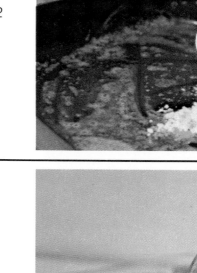

As the balls are browned, remove them from the skillet. When all are browned, add the last 2 tablespoons butter and melt, then stir in the flour and cook and stir until frothy.

Gradually add the coffee, boiling water and bouillon cube. Cook and stir until smooth and thickened, mashing the bouillon cube with the back of a spoon.

Return the meatballs to the skillet. Cover and simmer slowly for 25 to 30 minutes.

Swedish Meatballs

Moule au Fromage (Molded Cheese Loaf)

For a light but flavorful meatless entree, serve this delicate cheese loaf topped with Tomato Sauce, Creamed Mushrooms or fresh, sliced tomatoes. The numbered recipe directions tell how to make the recipe in the food processor. The photographed directions show how to make the same dish in a multipurpose machine like the Braun Kitchen Machine. The main difference between the two methods is that with the food processor all the ingredients, starting with the bread, go into the main processor container; with a multipurpose machine, such as the Braun model shown, some ingredients (starting with the cheese) are prepared in the blender and some in the mixing bowl.

2 slices firm white bread
12 ounces sharp Cheddar cheese, chilled
1 small onion, peeled and quartered
5 sprigs parsley
6 eggs
2 cups milk
¼ cup butter
1 teaspoon salt
¼ teaspoon dry mustard
3 cups cooked rice

1. Crumb the bread in the processor using the steel blade.
2. Cut the cheese into chunks and add them to the crumbs in the processor, along with the onion and parsley. Chop coarsely.
3. Add the eggs, milk, butter, salt and mustard. Process until smooth.
4. Measure the cooked rice into a mixing bowl. Pour the milk-egg mixture into the rice in the bowl and stir until mixed.
5. Pour the cheese and rice mixture into a buttered and paper-lined 9x5x3-inch loaf pan. Set the loaf pan in a 9x13x2-inch baking pan and pour hot water in the larger pan to a depth of 1 inch.
6. Bake the loaf in a preheated 350°F oven about 1 hour and 10 to 20 minutes, or until a knife inserted near the center comes out clean.
7. Turn the loaf out onto a heated serving platter and spoon Tomato Sauce or Creamed Mushrooms over the top, or serve with fresh, sliced tomatoes.

Makes 8 to 10 servings

Shred the cheese using a shredding blade or shredding attachment when making this cheese loaf in a multipurpose machine such as the Braun mixer shown.

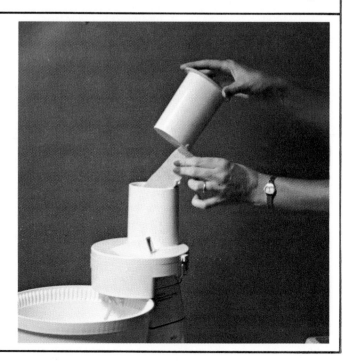

Tear the bread into several small pieces and make bread crumbs in the blender container. Add the crumbs to the cheese in the mixing bowl.

Quarter the onion and chop it in the blender container along with the parsley. Add it to the mixing bowl.

Break the eggs into the mixing bowl along with the cheese, onion and crumbs and beat slightly.

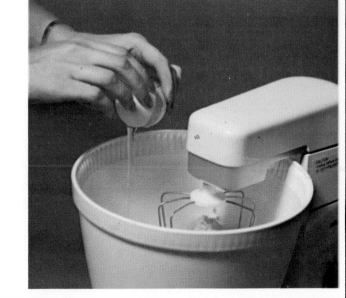

Heat the milk, butter and seasonings in a saucepan until the butter melts. Add the milk-butter mixture to the mixing bowl and beat until combined.

Add the rice and stir until combined.

Turn the mixture into a buttered and paper-lined 9x5x3-inch loaf pan.

Set the loaf pan in a 9x13x2-inch baking pan and pour hot water in the larger pan to a depth of 1 inch. Bake in preheated 350°F oven 1 hour and 10 to 20 minutes, or until a knife inserted near the center comes out clean.

Moule au Fromage (Molded Cheese Loaf)

Main Dishes

Ham 'N Swiss Pie

This is a hearty version of a quiche. Broccoli and ham are combined in the creamy cheese filling. A shredding blade can shred the cheese quickly. The rest of the ingredients can be prepared with the food processor's steel blade or multipurpose machine's blender.

4 ounces Swiss cheese, chilled
1 tablespoon flour
1 cup frozen chopped broccoli, thawed and drained
1 cup cooked ham or canned luncheon meat, cubed
9-inch pastry shell
1 cup milk
2 eggs
2 green onions, cut in short lengths
¼ teaspoon dry mustard
Dash salt
Dash pepper

1. Shred the cheese with a shredding blade and toss it with the flour.
2. Layer half the cheese, broccoli and ham in the pastry shell; then repeat the layers.
3. Combine the milk, eggs, onions and seasonings in the food processor or blender container. Blend until the onions are finely chopped.
4. Pour the sauce over the mixture in the pastry shell.
5. Bake it in a preheated 375°F oven 45 minutes or until a knife inserted near the center comes out clean.
6. Let the pie stand 5 minutes before cutting.

Makes 4 to 6 servings

Olympian Gold Sandwiches

These egg salad sandwiches are exceptionally tasty, thanks to the finely chopped vegetables. If you have the food processor, use the steel blade to chop the vegetables and eggs. If you have a multipurpose machine, prepare the recipe in the blender or use the slicing blade.

10 hard-cooked eggs
1 cucumber, peeled
1 tomato
2 carrots, cut in short lengths
2 stalks celery, cut in short lengths
2 green onions, cut in short lengths
½ cup bottled creamy French dressing
¼ teaspoon salt
6 Kaiser rolls or hard rolls
Mayonnaise or softened butter
Lettuce

1. Separately slice 2 of the eggs, the cucumber and the tomato in the food processor or blender. Set them aside.
2. Chop the remaining eggs and set them aside in a medium-sized bowl.
3. Chop the carrots, celery and onions with the French dressing and salt.
4. Add the vegetable-dressing mixture to the chopped eggs and stir until blended.
5. Cut each roll in half. Hollow out the centers of both halves of each roll with a fork, leaving a ½-inch shell.
6. Spread the mayonnaise or butter in the rolls.
7. Spread about ¼ cup egg salad mixture on each bottom roll half.
8. Top each of the bottom halves of the rolls with lettuce, a tomato slice, 2 cucumber slices and 2 egg slices each. Replace the tops.

Makes 6 sandwiches

Space Age Soufflé

A little heavier and creamier than the traditional soufflé, this contemporary quick soufflé is mixed all at once. It is fool-proof and wonderfully flavored with Cheddar and Parmesan cheese. Mix the entire recipe in the food processor (steel blade) or in a multipurpose machine's blender container.

1 tablespoon soft butter
¼ cup plus 2 tablespoons grated Parmesan cheese
6 eggs
½ cup dairy sour cream or light cream
½ teaspoon dry mustard
½ teaspoon salt
8 ounces sharp Cheddar cheese, cubed and chilled
1 package (8 ounces) cream cheese, cubed

1. Butter the bottom and sides of a 1- or 1¼-quart soufflé dish.
2. Sprinkle 2 tablespoons of the Parmesan cheese over the sides and bottom of the buttered dish. (Use more Parmesan, if necessary.)
3. Combine the eggs, sour or regular cream, the remaining ¼ cup Parmesan cheese and seasonings in the processor or blender. Blend about 15 seconds or until well combined.
4. With the motor running, add the cubes of Cheddar and cream cheese and blend about 20 to 30 seconds.
5. Pour into the Parmesan cheese-dusted dish.
6. Bake the soufflé in a preheated 375°F oven 45 to 50 minutes or until a knife inserted near the center comes out clean. Serve immediately.

Makes 4 to 6 servings

Broiled Fish with Deviled Cheese

Broiled Fish with Deviled Cheese

A spunky sauce makes broiled fish a special treat. This recipe is simple and quick enough to make after work. Use a shredding blade to quickly shred the cheese.

2 pounds fresh or frozen (thawed) fish fillets
  Butter, melted
4 ounces Cheddar cheese, chilled
2 tablespoons chili sauce
1 tablespoon prepared mustard
1½ teaspoons prepared horseradish

1. Arrange the fish fillets in a foil-covered broiling pan and brush with melted butter.
2. Broil several inches from heat for about 8 minutes or until the fish is lightly browned and flakes with a fork.
3. Shred the cheese with a shredding blade.
4. Mix the cheese, chili sauce, mustard and horseradish in a small bowl.
5. Spread the mixture over the fish.
6. Return the fish to the broiler for about 3 minutes or until the cheese melts and browns lightly.

Makes 4 to 6 servings

Quiche Lorraine

Whether you call it a "Quiche Lorraine" or a "cheese and bacon pie," this is a superb gourmet dish that is easy to make. Choose a slicing blade to slice the onions and select a shredding blade to quickly shred the cheese.

  9-inch unbaked pastry shell
8 slices bacon, cubed
1 medium onion, peeled and quartered
2 tablespoons flour
4 eggs
1 teaspoon salt
¼ teaspoon dry mustard
  Dash nutmeg
2 cups milk or light cream
6 ounces Cheddar, Swiss or Monterey Jack cheese, chilled

1. Bake the pastry shell in a preheated 425°F oven for 5 minutes.
2. Cook the bacon until crisp. Lift the bacon from the pan. Drain the drippings, and return 2 tablespoons of it to the pan.
3. Slice the onion with a slicing blade and add it to the drippings in the pan. Sauté about 2 minutes.
4. Sprinkle the flour over the onion. Stir to blend and cook briefly. Remove it from the heat, and set it aside.
5. Beat the eggs, seasonings, milk and sautéed onion in the food processor or blender just until they are combined.
6. Shred the cheese and arrange it in the pastry shell.
7. Pour the egg-milk mixture over the cheese; then sprinkle the bacon on top.
8. Bake in a preheated 350°F oven 35 to 45 minutes or until a knife inserted near the center comes out clean.
9. Let it stand 5 minutes before cutting into wedges.

Makes 6 servings

Tuna Mushroom Divan

With this stellar casserole in your recipe repertoire you can confidently volunteer to bring the main dish attraction to a potluck, picnic or party. You can bake the casserole ahead of time, then refrigerate and reheat it. Choose a slicing blade for the mushrooms, a shredding blade for the cheese and let the food processor's steel blade or a multipurpose machine's blender handle the chopping.

1 pound fresh mushrooms
5 tablespoons butter
1 medium onion, peeled and quartered
1 can (10½ ounces) condensed cream of mushroom soup
½ soup can of milk
1 teaspoon prepared mustard Dash white pepper
2 cans (6 to 7 ounces each) tuna, drained and flaked
2 or 3 sprigs parsley
2 cups uncooked medium egg noodles
½ teaspoon salt
1 bunch fresh broccoli, cut in spears, or 2 packages (10 ounces each) frozen broccoli spears
1 slice firm white bread, torn in pieces
1 ounce sharp Cheddar cheese, chilled

1. Rinse the mushrooms and cut off the tips of the stem ends. Slice the mushrooms with a slicing blade.
2. Melt 4 tablespoons of the butter in a large skillet.
3. Add the mushrooms and sauté 3 minutes. Remove half the mushrooms and set them aside.
4. Chop the onion medium-fine in the food processor (steel blade) or blender.
5. Add the onion, soup, milk, mustard and pepper to the skillet and mix well to make a sauce.
6. Stir in the tuna.
7. Chop the parsley in the food processor or blender and add it to the skillet. Set the skillet aside.
8. Cook the noodles according to the directions on the package. Drain; then stir in the remaining 1 tablespoon butter and the salt. Set the noodles aside.
9. Cook the broccoli in a small amount of boiling salted water, covered, about 10 minutes or until tender. (Cook frozen broccoli as the package directs.) Drain the broccoli.
10. Butter a 9x13x2-inch baking dish or 3-quart casserole. Layer half the noodles, all the broccoli, half the tuna-sauce mixture, the remaining noodles and the remaining tuna-sauce in the casserole.
11. Crumb the bread in the food processor (steel blade) or blender.
12. Shred the cheese with a shredding blade.
13. Combine the bread crumbs and cheese and scatter them around the edge of the casserole.
14. Arrange the reserved mushrooms in the center.
15. Bake in a preheated 375°F oven 15 minutes or until crumbs are golden and mixture is piping hot.
Note: You can prepare the casserole up to the point of baking, cover it and refrigerate. To bake, uncover the casserole, put it in a cold oven and set temperature at 375°F. Bake it about 45 minutes or until hot.

Makes 8 servings

Tuna Mushroom Divan   **Chicken With Mushrooms Mediterranean**

Crepes

These thin, tender French pancakes can wrap up an unbelievable variety of fillings. Mixing is quick and easy in the processor with the steel blade or in a blender.

 3 or 4 eggs
1½ cups milk
 3 tablespoons butter, melted
 1 cup all-purpose flour
 ½ teaspoon salt

1. Combine all the ingredients in the food processor or blender and blend until smooth.
2. Pour the batter into a jar or other container, cover and refrigerate at least 1 hour before baking. (The batter may be kept for a week in the refrigerator.)
3. To bake in a traditional pan, heat the pan until it will sizzle a drop of water.
4. Pour in just enough crepe batter to cover the bottom of the pan, tipping and tilting the pan to help swirl the batter over the bottom. (9-inch pans will take about 3 to 4 tablespoons of batter, 6-inch pans about 2 tablespoons of batter.) Pour off any excess batter.
5. Bake the crepes over medium-high heat until golden brown on the bottom and dry on top. Turn and brown the other side, if you wish, although it is necessary only for crepes that are not to be filled. Crepes for blintzes should only be browned on one side.
6. As the crepes are baked, stack them in a pie plate or deep plate and cover with a pan lid, foil or plastic wrap to keep them from drying out.
7. To bake on bottom-baking pans or other electric pans, follow the manufacturer's directions.

Makes about 3 cups batter

Variations: Add any of the following to the batter before blending: strips of the thin, outer portion of the peel of a lemon, lime or orange; ¼ cup grated Parmesan cheese; a handful of fresh herbs such as dill, parsley, or basil or ½ to 1 teaspoon of dried herbs; 1 packet of instant oatmeal.

Chicken with Mushrooms Mediterranean

This one-dish meal is rich in flavor, looks impressive and has only 334 calories per serving! The food processor's steel blade can coarsely chop the vegetables, or they can be sliced with the slicing blade of a multipurpose machine.

 1 pound fresh mushrooms
 1 (2½- to 3-pounds) chicken, cut into serving pieces
 1 teaspoon salt
 ¼ teaspoon pepper
 1 medium onion, peeled and quartered
 1 clove garlic
 1 can (1 pound) tomatoes
 2 teaspoons basil
 1 bay leaf
 3 medium zucchini, ends trimmed
 1 green pepper, seeded and quartered
 2 tablespoons flour

1. Rinse mushrooms; trim off the tips of the stems. Slice the mushrooms and set them aside.
2. Sprinkle the pieces of chicken with salt and pepper and arrange them on a rack in a 9x13x2-inch baking dish or pan. Bake them in a preheated 425°F oven 20 minutes.
3. Remove the pan from the oven. Remove the chicken; then pour off and discard the fat from the pan. Put the chicken pieces back into the pan without the rack. Lower the oven temperature to 350°F.
4. Chop the onion and garlic medium-fine in the food processor or blender and turn them into a large bowl along with the tomatoes and seasonings. Break the tomatoes into chunks with a spoon.
5. Coarsely chop the zucchini and green pepper by turning the food processor's motor on and off in short bursts; or slice them with the slicing blade of a multipurpose machine.
6. Add the zucchini, green peppers and mushrooms to the tomato mixture and combine.
7. Pour the tomato-vegetable mixture over the chicken in the pan. Cover and return the pan to the oven about 45 minutes or until the chicken is tender.
8. When the chicken is done, pour the liquid from the baking pan into a saucepan and sprinkle the flour over it. On top of the range, cook and stir the liquid and flour over medium-high heat until the mixture comes to a boil and is thickened.
9. Pour the sauce over the chicken in a heated serving dish or platter. Serve hot.

Makes 4 servings

Guacamole Crepes

You can wrap the mellow, rich avocado filling in small crepes to serve as appetizers, or you can fold the filling in larger crepes for a main dish. Guacamole is easy to prepare when you use the food processor's steel blade or a multipurpose machine's blender to blend the avocado and chop the vegetables. The lettuce and cheese can be shredded with a shredding blade.

2 medium avocados, peeled and pitted
2 to 3 tablespoons lemon juice
¼ small onion, peeled
½ teaspoon salt
Dash hot pepper sauce
6 large or 12 small crepes
1 medium tomato, peeled and quartered
¼ small head lettuce, quartered
2 ounces Cheddar cheese, chilled

1. Place the avocados in the food processor (steel blade) or blender with the lemon juice, onion, salt and hot pepper sauce. Blend until smooth and the onion is chopped.
2. Spread the mixture over the crepes and roll them up.
3. Coarsely chop the tomato in the food processor or blender and sprinkle over the filled crepes.
4. Shred the lettuce and cheese and sprinkle them over the crepes to serve.

Makes 12 appetizers or 6 main dish servings

Guacamole Crepes

Tailgate Chili

Battles are fought over the issue of beans or no beans in chili. This is a middle-of-the road chili with a moderate amount of beans and mild flavor. It is perfect to serve before or after a game, or on a picnic. The food processor's steel blade or a multipurpose machine's blender take care of the vegetable chopping chores.

2 medium onions, peeled and quartered
1 green pepper, seeded and quartered
2 pounds fresh pork sausage
2 cans (15 ounces each) kidney beans, drained
1 can (12 ounces) whole kernel corn, drained
1 can (15 ounces) tomato sauce
1 can (6 ounces) tomato paste
1 cup water
2 teaspoons chili powder
1 teaspoon salt

1. Chop the onions and pepper medium-fine and set them aside.
2. Brown the sausage in a large skillet or Dutch oven, breaking the sausage into small pieces with the back of a spoon as it browns.
3. Lift the sausage from the skillet with a slotted spoon and set it aside.
4. Pour off the drippings, reserving 3 tablespoons in the skillet.
5. Add the chopped vegetables to the reserved drippings and sauté 5 minutes over medium heat.
6. Add the sausage and all the remaining ingredients.
7. Simmer, covered, stirring occasionally, about 30 minutes.

Makes 6 to 8 servings

Tailgate Chili

Main Dishes

Old China Town Pork Burger

Oriental flavor takes on an American form in this robust sandwich. It is unusual enough for a special luncheon, and hearty enough for a family supper. Use the food processor's steel blade or the blender to chop the ingredients.

2 slices firm white bread, torn in chunks
4 green onions, cut in short lengths
½ medium green pepper, seeded
1 can (6½ ounces) water chestnuts, drained
1 pound pork sausage
1 egg
2 tablespoons dry sherry
2 tablespoons soy sauce
1 small clove garlic, crushed
¼ teaspoon ground ginger
6 large enriched sesame-seed hamburger buns
   Butter
1 cup bean sprouts, rinsed and well-drained
   Sweet and Sour Sauce

1. Put the bread in the food processor or blender and make bread crumbs. Pour the crumbs into a large bowl.
2. Finely chop the green onions; add them to the bread crumbs.
3. Finely chop the pepper and water chestnuts and add them to the bread crumbs.
4. Add the sausage, egg, sherry, soy sauce, garlic and ginger and mix well. Chill the mixture several hours for easier handling, if you wish.
5. Shape the burger mixture into 6 patties and grill until done.
6. Split, toast and butter the buns.
7. Divide the bean sprouts on the bottom halves of the buns and top each with a patty.
8. Spoon equal amounts of Sweet and Sour Sauce over each patty. Close sandwiches with top of bun.

Makes 6 sandwiches

Sweet and Sour Sauce
½ cup crushed pineapple, drained
⅓ cup catsup
2 tablespoons vinegar
2 tablespoons orange marmalade
1 tablespoon prepared mustard

1. Combine all the ingredients in a small saucepan.
2. Heat the mixture until the marmalade melts.

Makes about 1 cup

Old China Town Pork Burger

Hawaiian Salmon Patties

For a spur-of-the moment treat, you can mix together these broiled salmon patties. Served with rice, they make a delicious instant main dish. The patties can be made in the food processor (steel blade) or multipurpose machine's blender.

8 square soda crackers
1 small onion, peeled and quartered
1 can (16 ounces) salmon, drained
1 egg
¼ teaspoon salt
¼ teaspoon dill weed
Dash pepper
6 slices pineapple

1. Make cracker crumbs in the food processor or blender. Measure ½ cup crumbs and place them in a medium-sized bowl; set it aside.
2. Chop the onion medium-fine in the food processor or blender.
3. Add the salmon and turn the motor on and off quickly to break the salmon into large pieces.
4. Add the salmon and onion to the cracker crumbs, along with the egg, salt, dill weed, and pepper and mix lightly.
5. Form the mixture into 6 patties and place each on a pineapple slice.
6. Broil about 3 inches from heat about 10 minutes or until the patties are brown. Turn and broil about 8 minutes longer or until the pineapple is brown.

Makes 6 servings

Meat Loaf à la Roma

A savory meat loaf with a Roman flair, you can add the Italian accent with premixed seasonings or use any combination of oregano, thyme, marjoram and basil that you prefer. The food processor's steel blade can do a quick job on the beef — be careful not to overprocess. If you have a multipurpose machine, use its grinder attachment to grind the meat. The food processor's steel blade or the multipurpose machine's blender can make the bread crumbs and chop the vegetables.

5 slices day-old bread, torn in pieces
1 clove garlic
2 pounds lean, tender beef, cubed
1 onion, peeled and quartered
½ green pepper, halved and seeded
¼ cup beef bouillon
½ cup catsup, divided
2 tablespoons horseradish
2 teaspoons salt
1 teaspoon Italian herb seasoning
½ teaspoon dry mustard
½ teaspoon pepper

1. Place the bread and the garlic in the food processor or blender container and make coarse bread crumbs. Measure 2 cups crumbs. Set them aside.
2. Grind the beef medium-coarse, a pound at a time, in the food processor (steel blade) or in a meat grinder. (Turn the motor of the food processor on and off quickly to make a medium-coarse grind.) Set it aside.
3. Chop the onion and green pepper in the food processor or blender container.
4. In a large bowl, combine the bread crumbs, onion, green pepper, beef bouillon, ¼ cup catsup, horseradish, salt, Italian seasoning, mustard and pepper. Add the ground beef and mix lightly.
5. Pack the mixture into a 9x5x3-inch loaf pan.
6. Spread the remaining ¼ cup catsup on top of the loaf.
7. Bake the loaf in a preheated 350°F oven 1¼ hours.

Makes 8 servings

Timbales Jambon (Ham Timbales)

This gourmet dish is the thrifty chef's secret for using leftover ham. You could replace the ham with a comparable amount of cooked turkey, chicken, chicken livers, shrimp or crabmeat. The food processor's steel blade or a multipurpose machine's blender can handle the chopping. The shredding blade of either type of machine will quickly shred the cheese.

1 ounce Swiss cheese, chilled
6 ounces cooked ham, cubed
4 eggs
1 slice onion, 1-inch thick
½ teaspoon paprika
1 cup milk, scalded

1. Shred the cheese; place 1 tablespoon of cheese in each of four 9-ounce custard cups.
2. Place the ham in the food processor or blender. Turn the motor on and off quickly, just until the ham is chopped.
3. Place about ¼ cup of ham in each custard cup, over the cheese.
4. Blend the eggs, onion and paprika just until the onion is chopped.
5. Slowly pour in the milk while the machine is running.
6. Pour the mixture over the ham and cheese in the custard cups.
7. Set the cups in a large baking pan; pour very hot water into the pan to within ½ inch of the top of the custard mixture.
8. Bake in a preheated 350°F oven 40 to 45 minutes or until a knife inserted near the center comes out clean.
9. Remove the cups from the hot water; gently loosen the custard at the top with a spatula and invert on serving plates.

Makes 4 servings

Cheese Soufflé

Cheese Soufflé

This high-rising beauty will win accolades from your gourmet friends. You will have to beat the egg whites in a mixer to make the soufflé light and fluffy. The food processor can be used to grate the Parmesan cheese (steel blade), shred the Cheddar cheese (shredding blade), chop the onion (steel blade) and beat the egg yolks (plastic blade). If you have a multipurpose machine, use its blender to grate the Parmesan cheese, then turn to the shredding blade for the Cheddar cheese. The blender can also be used to chop the onion and beat the egg yolks.

1	ounce Parmesan cheese, chilled
4	ounces Cheddar cheese, chilled
1	slice onion, ½-inch thick
⅓	cup butter
⅓	cup all-purpose flour
½	teaspoon dry mustard
1½	cups milk
6	eggs, separated
¼	teaspoon cream of tartar

1. Grate the Parmesan cheese in the food processor (steel blade) or in a blender.
2. Butter a 2½-quart soufflé dish or casserole. Dust it with the grated cheese. Set it aside.
3. Finely shred the Cheddar cheese with a shredding blade. Set it aside.
4. Chop the onion in the food processor or blender.
5. Sauté the onion in the butter in a medium saucepan for 5 minutes.
6. Stir in the flour and dry mustard. Cook and stir until smooth and bubbly.
7. Add the milk all at once. Cook and stir over medium-high heat until the mixture comes to a boil and is smooth and thick. Remove the saucepan from the heat.
8. Stir in the reserved Cheddar cheese; stir until it melts.
9. Beat the egg yolks in the food processor (plastic blade) or blender until thick and lemon-colored.
10. Stir a small amount of the hot cheese mixture into the yolks. Return the yolk mixture to the saucepan and blend.
11. Using a mixer, beat the egg whites and cream of tartar in a mixing bowl until stiff but not dry, just until whites no longer slip when bowl is tilted.
12. Gently fold the yolk mixture into the whites.
13. Pour the egg mixture into the prepared dish.
14. Holding a spoon upright, make a ring 1 inch deep and 1 inch from side of dish.
15. Bake the soufflé in a preheated 350°F oven 35 to 40 minutes or until puffy and delicately browned; soufflé should only shake slightly when the oven rack is gently moved back and forth. Serve it immediately.

Makes 6 servings

Mideastern Kibbee

Kibbee is a wonderfully spicy Mideastern dish that includes cracked wheat, lamb, beef, peanuts and raisins. Try serving it with a side dish of cucumbers in yogurt. If you are using the food processor, let the steel blade grind the meats and do the chopping. If you have multipurpose machine, let the meat grinder do the grinding and the blender container can be used to do the chopping. The shredding blade of either kind of machine can shred the carrot.

1 cup cracked wheat (bulgar wheat)
1 cup dry white wine
2 medium onions, peeled and quartered
¾ pound lean, boneless lamb, cubed
2½ teaspoons salt, divided
Pepper to taste
2 to 3 sprigs parsley
2 pounds lean, boneless beef, cubed
1 cup salted shelled peanuts, divided
1¼ cups golden raisins, divided
1 teaspoon allspice
1 teaspoon coriander
¼ pound butter
1 medium carrot, cut in short lengths

1. Combine the wheat and wine in a small saucepan; let it stand 30 minutes.
2. Cook the wheat over medium heat until the wine is absorbed.
3. Chop the onions in the food processor or blender. Set them aside.
4. Grind the lamb in the food processor or grinder. Combine the lamb, wheat mixture, half of the chopped onions, 1½ teaspoons of the salt and the pepper; set this aside.
5. Chop the parsley in the food processor or blender.
6. Grind the beef in the food processor or grinder. Combine the beef with the remaining chopped onion, parsley, ½ cup of the peanuts, 1 cup of the golden raisins, allspice, coriander, and remaining 1 teaspoon salt.
7. Melt the butter in a large skillet; add the beef mix mixture and cook until the butter is absorbed.
8. Spread the beef mixture on a large oven-proof platter or in a 9x13x2-inch baking dish. Cover with the lamb mixture and the remaining ½ cup peanuts.
9. Bake in a preheated 350°F oven 1 hour.
10. Shred the carrot; sprinkle the carrot and the remaining raisins over the hot Kibbee before serving.

Makes 8 to 10 servings

Mideastern Kibbee

Omelettes Elegant

Omelettes made in the food processor or blender are marvelously light. The creamy filling in these omelettes combines Parmesan cheese and broccoli. The recipe is quickly made in the food processor (steel blade) or in a multipurpose machine's blender.

1 ounce Parmesan cheese
1 pound fresh broccoli, cooked, well-drained and cut into 1-inch pieces
1 package (3 ounces) cream cheese, cubed
1 tablespoon lemon juice
¼ teaspoon seasoned salt
6 eggs
⅓ cup water
½ teaspoon salt
   Dash pepper
3 tablespoons butter, divided
1 medium tomato, sliced

1. Grate the Parmesan cheese in the food processor (steel blade) or blender. Set it aside.
2. Place the broccoli, a small amount at a time, in the food processor or blender. Turn the motor on and off quickly until the broccoli is coarsely chopped.
3. Put the broccoli in a medium-sized saucepan as each batch is chopped.
4. Combine the cream cheese, reserved Parmesan cheese, lemon juice and seasoned salt in the food processor or blender. Blend until combined.
5. Stir the cheese mixture into the broccoli in the saucepan to make the filling. Keep the filling warm while preparing the omelettes.
6. Combine the eggs, water, salt and pepper in the food processor or blender container. Blend until combined.
7. For each omelette, melt 1 tablespoon butter in an omelette pan or skillet until it is just hot enough to sizzle a drop of water.
8. Pour in about ½ cup of the omelette mixture. The mixture's edges should set at once.
9. With a pancake turner, carefully draw the cooked portions of the edges toward the center, so uncooked portions flow to the bottom.
10. Tilt the pan if necessary to make the uncooked portions flow to the edges.
11. Slide the pan rapidly back and forth over heat to keep mixture in motion and sliding freely.
12. While the top is still moist and creamy-looking, place about ⅔ cup broccoli mixture on half of the omelette.
13. Top with 2 to 3 tomato slices.
14. With the pancake turner, fold the omelette in half, turning it out onto a plate with a quick flip of the wrist.
15. Keep the omelette warm while preparing remaining omelettes.

Makes 3 servings

Chinese Beef and Celery

Crisp-tender vegetables, thin-sliced meat and a perfectly seasoned sauce make a superb Oriental dish to be served over rice. You can do all the slicing with the food processor's steel blade. Some multipurpose machines do not recommend slicing raw meat, so check the instructions of your machine — you may have to slice the meat by hand and use the slicing blade for the vegetables only.

2 pounds beef flank steak
1 head celery, top trimmed, cut in short lengths
3 green onions, cut in short lengths
2 medium carrots, cut in short lengths
2 tablespoons oil
1 clove garlic, minced
2½ tablespoons cornstarch
¼ cup soy sauce
1 beef bouillon cube
½ cup boiling water
1 can (1 pound) bean sprouts, drained
2 teaspoons sugar
½ teaspoon ground ginger

1. Freeze the steak until firm but not solid, about 30 to 45 minutes. Cut it into pieces to just fit into the feeder tube of the food processor or slicing attachment and slice. Remove the slices and set them aside.
2. Slice the celery with a slicing blade; set it aside.
3. Slice the green onions and set them aside.
4. Slice the carrots; set them aside.
5. Heat the oil in a wok or large skillet.
6. Add the beef slices, a few at a time, and brown over high heat.
7. Add the celery, onions and garlic; cook and stir 2 minutes.
8. Blend the cornstarch and soy sauce.
9. Dissolve the bouillon cube in boiling water.
10. Add the cornstarch mixture, bouillon, bean sprouts, carrots, sugar and ginger to the wok and mix.
11. Heat to boiling; then reduce the heat, cover and simmer about 5 to 7 minutes or until the vegetables are crisp-tender.

Makes 6 servings

Orange Raisin Stuffed Lamb Roll

A flavorful stuffing and a marvelous Orange Mint Sauce can make a lamb roast the star attraction for your next dinner party. The food processor's steel blade or a multipurpose machine's blender can do all the chopping.

1 (6-pounds) leg of lamb, boned and butterflied
Salt
Pepper
1 medium to large onion, peeled and quartered
3 tablespoons butter
4 to 6 stalks celery, cut in short lengths
2 oranges
10 slices cinnamon raisin bread, cut into small cubes
1 egg, beaten
Orange Mint Sauce

1. Flatten the leg of lamb with a mallet. Sprinkle it with salt and pepper and set aside.
2. Chop the onion medium-fine in the blender or food processor and turn it into a saucepan or skillet with the butter.
3. Chop the celery medium-fine and add to the saucepan with the onion.
4. Sauté the vegetables about 5 minutes or until they are tender.
5. Cut the thin, outer portion of peel from the oranges with a knife or vegetable peeler. Grate the peel in the food processor or blender.
6. Combine the grated peel, bread, egg and sautéed vegetables in a large bowl and toss lightly to mix.
7. Spread the stuffing over the lamb and roll it up in a jelly roll fashion. Tie it with a string.
8. Put the rolled roast on a rack in a shallow roasting pan and roast in a preheated 350°F oven 2 hours for medium-rare.
9. Reserve the drippings in the pan for the Orange Mint Sauce.
10. Remove the roast to a heated platter and slice. Spoon Orange Mint Sauce over it to serve.

Makes 6 to 8 servings

Orange Mint Sauce
2 oranges
1¾ cups orange juice
⅓ cup brown sugar
¼ cup butter
1 tablespoon cornstarch
1 tablespoon dried mint flakes, crushed
1½ teaspoons ground ginger
1 teaspoon ground cloves
2 teaspoons salt

1. Cut the thin, outer portion of peel from the oranges with a knife or vegetable peeler.
2. Grate the peel in the food processor or blender. Turn it into the roasting pan with the lamb drippings.
3. Cut the white portion of the peel from the oranges and discard. Section the oranges and set them aside.
4. Add all the remaining ingredients to the roasting pan.
5. Cook over medium heat, stirring to loosen the crusty bits from the pan, until mixture comes to a boil and is smooth and thickened.
6. Stir in the orange sections; then pour the sauce into a gravy boat or serving dish to pass with the Orange Raisin Stuffed Lamb Roll.

Makes about 2 cups

Chinese Beef and Celery   Orange Raisin Stuffed Lamb Roll

Bombay Ham Crepes

Ham, chutney and pineapple make an exotic filling for crepes. The whole recipe can be prepared in a few minutes, if you have made your crepes ahead of time. The food processor's steel blade or a multipurpose machine's blender can chop the chutney. The cheese can be shredded quickly with a shredding blade.

1 can (1 pound, 4 ounces) pineapple chunks 1 tablespoon cornstarch 1 teaspoon curry powder 2 cups cubed cooked ham 1 tablespoon lemon or lime juice ¼ cup chutney 8 large crepes 4 ounces Cheddar cheese, chilled	1. Drain the pineapple chunks, reserving the syrup. 2. Blend the syrup, cornstarch and curry powder in a saucepan. 3. Cook and stir over medium heat until the mixture comes to a boil and is smooth and thickened. 4. Add the ham and lemon juice and heat until piping hot. 5. Finely chop the chutney in the food processor or blender; add it to the saucepan. Remove it from the heat. 6. Spoon about ⅓ cup of the filling down the center of each crepe. 7. Roll up or fold the crepes and arrange them on a heat-proof platter, or in a greased 9x13x2-inch baking dish or pan. 8. Spoon any remaining filling over the top. 9. Shred the cheese and sprinkle it over the crepes. 10. Broil about 5 to 6 inches from the heat until the cheese melts.

Makes 4 to 8 servings

Chicken Breasts Mirepoix

Chicken and vegetables are especially delicious when they are baked together. Try serving this flavorful dish with rice pilaf. The slicing blade of the food processor or multipurpose machine can handle all the vegetables in no time.

3 tablespoons flour 1¼ teaspoons salt ¼ teaspoon pepper 6 chicken breasts, boned 2 tablespoons oil 6 stalks celery, cut in short lengths 2 medium carrots, cut in short lengths 2 medium onions, peeled and quartered 2 tablespoons butter 1 chicken bouillon cube ½ cup boiling water	1. Stir together the flour, salt and pepper. Coat the chicken pieces with the seasoned flour. 2. Heat the oil in a large skillet. Add the chicken and brown about 3 minutes on each side. Set the chicken aside. 3. Slice the celery, carrots and onions with a slicing blade. 4. Melt the butter in the same skillet. Add the sliced vegetables and sauté them about 3 minutes. 5. Dissolve the bouillon cube in boiling water and add it to the celery mixture. 6. Spoon the vegetables into a shallow 2-quart casserole and arrange the chicken pieces on top. 7. Cover and bake in a preheated 350°F oven about 30 minutes or until the chicken is tender.

Makes 6 servings

Deviled Cheese Sandwiches

The soft filling is a devilishly good contrast to the crispy grilled bread. Prepare the filling in advance, if you like. The food processor's steel blade or a multipurpose machine's blender can do the chopping and mixing. The shredding blade of any machine can handle the cheese.

4 hard-cooked eggs, halved ¼ cup mayonnaise or salad dressing 1 green onion, cut in short lengths 1 large sprig parsley 1 (1-inch) strip whole pimiento 1 teaspoon prepared mustard ¼ teaspoon Worcestershire sauce ¼ teaspoon salt 2 ounces Cheddar cheese, chilled Softened butter 8 slices bread	1. Place the eggs, mayonnaise, onion, parsley, pimiento, mustard, Worcestershire sauce and salt in the food processor or blender. Turn the motor on and off quickly just until the eggs are chopped. 2. Shred the cheese with a shredding blade. 3. Stir the cheese into the egg mixture. 4. Butter one side of the bread slices. 5. Turn over 4 slices of bread and spread each with about ⅓ cup egg-and-cheese mixture. 6. Top them with the remaining slices of bread, buttered-side up. 7. Grill the sandwiches in a skillet or on a griddle until toasted on both sides or place the sandwiches on a baking sheet and bake in a preheated 400°F oven 5 to 8 minutes on each side or until golden brown.

Makes 4 sandwiches

Mediterranean Seawich

A very classy version of a tuna salad sandwich, this unique lunch or supper special features shrimp, mushrooms and a pretty sliced-egg garnish. Let the slicing blade of any machine handle the celery and olives. Turn to a shredding blade for the cheese.

2 stalks celery, cut in short lengths
10 medium pimiento-stuffed green olives
8 ounces canned small shrimp
1 can (7 ounces) tuna, drained and flaked
1 can (2 ounces) mushroom stems and pieces, drained
¼ cup mayonnaise
1 tablespoon lemon juice
6 slices dark rye bread
    Butter
6 ounces Cheddar cheese, chilled
6 hard-cooked eggs, sliced

1. Slice the celery and olives with a slicing blade and turn into a medium-sized bowl.
2. Add the shrimp, tuna, mushrooms, mayonnaise and lemon juice and mix well. Chill until ready to serve.
3. Butter the bread and divide the tuna mixture among the slices, spreading it to the edges.
4. Shred the cheese with a shredding blade.
5. Arrange the egg slices on each sandwich; then sprinkle each sandwich with shredded cheese. Serve with a knife and fork.

Makes 6 sandwiches

Mediterranean Seawich

Pizza

A chewy crust and a savory topping make a pizza with pizzaz! You will be amazed at how quickly you can make dough in the food processor. If you have a multipurpose machine, it can cut down all or most of the kneading. When ready, the dough will make a ball and clean the sides of the bowl. The shredding and slicing blades of either type of machine can be used to prepare the cheese and onion.

1 package active dry yeast
⅔ cup warm water
2 cups all-purpose flour
½ teaspoon salt
2 tablespoons oil
12 ounces mozzarella cheese, chilled
1 small onion, peeled and quartered
¼ pound mushrooms
2 tablespoons butter
½ to ⅔ cup tomato sauce
Oregano
Thyme
Garlic salt
Anchovies (optional)

1. Dissolve the yeast in water in a small bowl.
2. Combine the flour and salt in the food processor or mixing bowl of a multipurpose machine.
3. Add the yeast and oil; blend until smooth and the dough begins to form a ball and leaves the side of the bowl or food processor's container.
4. Turn dough out onto a lightly floured surface and knead 2 to 3 minutes.
5. Place the dough in a greased bowl. Turn the dough to grease the top. Cover the dough and let it rise in a warm place about 2 hours or until it is doubled in bulk.
6. Pat and stretch the dough to fit a 12-inch pizza pan.
7. Shred the cheese and set it aside.
8. Slice the onion and mushrooms.
9. Melt the butter in a skillet. Add the onion and mushrooms and sauté until tender.
10. Spread the tomato sauce over the dough. Sprinkle with the cheese, onion, mushrooms, oregano, thyme, garlic salt and anchovies, if desired.
11. Bake in a preheated 400°F oven 25 minutes.

Makes one 12-inch pizza

Note: The completed pizza may be frozen up to one week before baking.

Cajun Cheese Soufflé

Soufflé with a southern accent, Cajun Cheese Soufflé has green pepper and bacon adding color and flavor. The pepper can be chopped with the food processor's steel blade or in the blender of a multipurpose machine. The shredding blade of either kind of machine makes quick work of shredding the cheese.

¼ cup butter
¼ cup all-purpose flour
1½ cups milk, scalded
¼ teaspoon salt
Dash cayenne pepper
½ pound Cheddar cheese, chilled
4 eggs, separated
¼ pound bacon, cut into short lengths
1 green pepper, seeded and halved

1. Melt the butter in a saucepan. Add the flour and cook and stir until bubbly. Add the milk; cook and stir until smooth and thickened to make a cream sauce. Stir in the salt and cayenne pepper. Remove the saucepan from the heat.
2. Shred the cheese in the food processor or blender.
3. Add the cheese to the cream sauce and stir until it has melted. Stir in the egg yolks, one at a time. Cover the pan and set it aside.
4. Fry the bacon until crisp and drain it on absorbent paper. Reserve the fat.
5. Chop one half of the green pepper, using the steel blade of the food processor or blender. Slice the remaining half, using the slicing blade.
6. Sauté the chopped green pepper in the reserved bacon fat until tender; then drain it on absorbent paper.
7. Stir the chopped green pepper and ¾ of the bacon into the cheese mixture.
8. Beat the egg whites with a mixer until stiff. Gently fold them into the cheese mixture. Turn into a 2-quart straight-sided casserole or soufflé dish.
9. Bake in a preheated 375°F oven 30 to 45 minutes.
10. Garnish the soufflé with the remaining chopped bacon and sliced green pepper.

Makes 6 servings

Pizza

Cajun Cheese Soufflé

Ham Loaf

For a robust, satisfying main dish there is nothing better than this old-fashioned Ham Loaf. You may want to buy a bigger-than-usual ham for a special dinner so you will have enough leftovers to make this loaf. The steel blade of the food processor or the meat grinder of a multipurpose machine can grind the ingredients.

1 pound smoked cooked ham, cubed
1 pound lean, boneless pork, cubed
1 medium onion, peeled and quartered
3 slices whole-wheat or rye bread, torn in pieces
4 sweet pickles
4 eggs

1. Place all the ingredients in the food processor and mix until the meat is finely chopped and all ingredients are thoroughly combined. Or, grind all the ingredients in a grinder and then mix them well by hand or with a mixer.
2. Pack the mixture into a 8½ x 4½ -inch loaf pan and bake it in a preheated 350°F oven about 1¼ hours.

Makes 6 to 8 servings

Crown Roast of Lamb with Fruit Stuffing

Here is a main dish fit for a royal banquet. The tartness of the apricots and the colors of the fruits make this stuffing a perfect match for the lamb. Use the steel blade of the food processor or a multipurpose machine's blender to chop the fruits, vegetables and nuts.

1 (5 to 6 pounds) crown roast of lamb

1. Preheat the oven to 450°F. Place the crown roast of lamb on a rack in a shallow pan. Cover the tips of the bones with foil. Immediately after putting the meat in the oven, reduce heat to 350°F. Roast the lamb 30 minutes to the pound for well-done (175-180°F) or 20 to 25 minutes per pound for medium-rare (160-165°F). Do not cover or baste.
2. When one hour of cooking time remains, remove the lamb roast from the oven and fill the center with 3 cups of Fruit Stuffing. Return the roast to the oven and complete the cooking. Carve, allowing 2 ribs per person.

Makes 6 to 7 servings

Fruit Stuffing
- ½ cup dried prunes
- ⅓ cup dried apricots
- 1 cup lukewarm water
- ½ cup pecans
- 2 stalks celery, cut in short lengths
- 1 onion, peeled and quartered
- 1 apple, cored and quartered
- ½ cup butter or margarine
- 1 package (14 ounces) seasoned bread cubes

1. Combine the prunes and apricots with water in the food processor or blender and coarsely chop.
2. Place the fruit in a saucepan and simmer 5 minutes; cool, and then drain.
3. Coarsely chop (but do not combine) the nuts, celery, onion and apples.
4. Sauté the onion and celery in the butter until tender. Add the apples and nuts.
5. Toss the fruit with 1 quart seasoned bread cubes. Measure 3 cups stuffing to fill crown roast of lamb. Place remaining stuffing in another pan. Cover and bake along with meat for 1 hour.

Rotini con Due Fromaggi (Rotini with Two Cheeses)

Serve this elegant, savory version of macaroni and cheese with a crisp vegetable salad for a delicious light supper. The steel blade of the food processor or a multipurpose machine's blender can do all the chopping. Turn to a slicing blade for neatly sliced mushrooms and let a shredding blade handle the cheese.

- 2 to 3 parsley sprigs
- 3 green onions, cut in short lengths
- 1 jar (4 ounces) pimientos, drained
- ½ pound fresh mushrooms
- 4 ounces Swiss cheese, chilled
- 4 ounces Cheddar cheese, chilled
- 3 quarts water
- 1½ tablespoons salt
- 12 ounces enriched durum rotini
- ¼ cup butter
- ¼ cup all-purpose flour
- 1 tablespoon seasoned salt
- 2 teaspoons dry mustard
- ¼ teaspoon white pepper
- 3½ cups milk
- 1 tablespoon Worcestershire sauce

1. Chop the parsley in the food processor or blender; set it aside.
2. Chop the onions and pimientos in the food processor or blender; set them aside.
3. Slice the mushrooms with the slicing blade and set them aside.
4. Shred both cheeses with the shredding blade; set them aside.
5. Measure 3 quarts water into a large pot or kettle; add salt and heat to boiling.
6. Add the rotini and cook until not quite tender, about 6 to 7 minutes. Drain.
7. Meanwhile, melt the butter in a medium-sized saucepan.
8. Add the flour, seasoned salt, dry mustard and pepper and cook and stir over medium heat until bubbly.
9. Add the milk and cook and stir until mixture comes to a boil and is smooth and thickened.
10. Stir in the shredded cheeses, chopped parsley, sliced mushrooms, chopped onions, pimiento and the Worcestershire sauce; cook and stir until the cheeses melt.
11. Combine the cheese sauce and rotini.
12. Turn into a greased 2-quart baking dish or casserole.
13. Bake in a preheated 350°F oven 45 to 50 minutes.

Makes 6 to 8 servings

Rotini con Due Fromaggi (Rotini with Two Cheeses)

Baked Cheddar Fondue

Baked Cheddar Fondue

This beautiful, light main dish is impressive to look at, and as easy to put together as an ordinary cheese sandwich. Shred the cheese with the shredding blade of the food processor, or mix the ingredients in the blender container of a multipurpose machine. Separate directions are given for the food processor and multipurpose machines.

6 slices white bread, halved
    diagonally
6 eggs
3 cups milk
4 ounces Cheddar cheese, chilled
½ teaspoon salt
½ teaspoon dry mustard

Food Processor Method
1. Arrange the bread slices in a pinwheel in a buttered 9-inch pie plate or baking dish.
2. Beat the eggs and milk.
3. Shred the cheese.
4. Add half of the cheese to the egg-milk mixture along with the salt and dry mustard.
5. Pour it over the bread.
6. Sprinkle the remaining cheese over the top.
Bake in a preheated 350°F oven about 40 minutes or until a knife inserted near the center comes out clean. Serve at once.

Multipurpose Machine Method
1. Arrange the bread slices in a pinwheel in a buttered 9-inch pie plate or baking dish.
2. Combine the eggs, milk, all of the cheese and seasonings in the blender and blend until the cheese is coarsely chopped.
3. Pour the mixture over the bread.
4. Bake in a preheated 350°F oven about 40 minutes or until a knife inserted near the center comes out clean. Serve at once.   *Makes 6 servings*

Quick Main Dish Ideas

Start with a basic Quiche mixture of 4 eggs, 1½ cups light cream or half-and-half, 2 to 4 ounces of shredded cheese and then add anything you like. You might finely chop (in a blender or food processor) a cup of leftover cooked vegetables or meat; slice and partially cook a small zucchini; crisp-cook and crumble some bacon; brown and crumble

sausage or ground beef; shred some carrots. Pour the filling into a 9-inch pie shell. Makes 6 servings.

If you have just a little cooked meat or poultry on hand, you can turn it into a super sandwich spread. Finely chop enough meat to make about 1 cup and then blend it along with ⅓ cup mayonnaise, a few chunks of celery

or green pepper, some nuts and salt and pepper to taste. Simple! Makes about 1⅓ cups.

Stuffing for a big bird is simple with a slicing blade in the food processor or other machines. Use the slicing blade for the onions, celery, apples and chestnuts. Then switch to the steel blade or blender to make bread crumbs of dry white or whole wheat bread, corn bread or raisin bread for the stuffing base.

Goober Casserole

Peanuts add surprisingly good flavor, crunch and protein to this delicious baked dish. The food processor's steel blade or the blender of a multipurpose machine can quickly chop the vegetables and peanuts. Turn to a shredding blade to handle the cheese.

1	medium onion, peeled and quartered
½	green pepper, seeded
1	cup salted peanuts
1	jar (2 ounces) pimiento, drained
4	ounces Cheddar cheese, chilled
3	tablespoons butter
3	tablespoons flour
1	teaspoon salt
½	teaspoon dry mustard
2	cups milk
8	ounces spaghetti

1. Chop the onion and green pepper medium-fine in the food processor (steel blade) or blender. Set them aside.
2. Coarsely chop the peanuts; set them aside.
3. Chop the pimiento medium-fine; set it aside.
4. Shred the cheese with a shredding blade and set it aside.
5. Melt the butter in a medium-sized saucepan. Add the onion and pepper and sauté over medium-high heat about 5 minutes.
6. Stir in the flour, salt and mustard and cook and stir until bubbly.
7. Add the milk and cook and stir until the mixture comes to a boil and is smooth and thickened. Remove the saucepan from the heat.
8. Cook the spaghetti in boiling salted water until just tender, about 5 to 6 minutes. Drain.
9. Arrange the spaghetti in a greased 1½-quart casserole or baking dish.
10. Pour the sauce over the spaghetti. Sprinkle with the cheese, peanuts and pimiento.
11. Bake in a preheated 350°F oven 30 minutes or until the top is lightly browned.

Makes 4 to 6 servings

Goober Casserole

Welsh Rarebit

The secret to velvet-smooth Welsh Rarebit is to stir the beer and cheese constantly over low heat until they are thoroughly blended. Welsh Rarebit makes a lovely light supper served with English muffins and a side dish of sliced fresh tomatoes. The shredding blade of any machine will quickly shred the cheese.

8 ounces Cheshire or Cheddar
    cheese, chilled
½ cup beer
    Dash Worcestershire sauce
    Dash paprika
    Dash pepper
1 egg yolk
2 tomatoes, peeled
4 English muffins, split and
    toasted

1. Shred the cheese with a shredding blade.
2. Place the cheese and beer in a saucepan. Warm it over low heat until the cheese melts; stir it constantly until the mixture becomes smooth and begins to thicken.
3. Add the Worcestershire sauce, paprika and pepper.
4. Stir in the egg yolk and cook over low heat until thickened and smooth — about 5 minutes.
5. Cut the tomatoes into wedges and stir them into the cheese mixture.
6. To serve, spoon the sauce over the English muffins.

Makes 4 servings

Ringtum Ditty

An extra quick version of Welsh Rarebit, this easy dish is excellent for school-day lunches or late-night suppers. The steel blade of the food processor or a multipurpose machine's blender can chop the onions; a shredding blade can handle the cheese.

2 medium onions, peeled and
    quartered
¼ cup butter
1 pound sharp Cheddar cheese,
    chilled
1 can (10½ ounces) condensed
    cream of tomato soup
1 egg, slightly beaten
½ teaspoon Worcestershire sauce
    Dash cayenne pepper
    Toast cups or crackers

1. Finely chop the onions in the food processor (steel blade) or blender.
2. Melt the butter in a skillet. Add the onions and sauté until they are tender.
3. Shred the cheese and add it to the skillet, along with the soup. Cook and stir over low heat until the cheese melts.
4. Stir a small amount of the cheese mixture into the beaten egg. Return the whole egg mixture to the skillet, along with the Worcestershire sauce and cayenne pepper.
5. Heat just until piping hot, but do not boil.
6. Spoon the cheese mixture into toast cups or over crackers to serve. Refrigerate any leftovers; to reheat, stir constantly over low heat.

Makes 8 servings

Beef and Mushroom Ratatouille

A one-dish meal, this savory mixture is based on the flavorful Mediterranean vegetable dish of ratatouille. The food processor's steel blade can be used for the chopping and its slicing blade for the slicing. If you have a multipurpose machine, chop the vegetables in the blender and do the slicing with the slicing blade.

1 tablespoon oil
2½ pounds lean boneless beef
    shoulder or chuck, cut in 1½-
    inch cubes
2 medium onions, peeled and
    quartered
1 clove garlic
1 can (1 pound, 12 ounces)
    tomatoes
1 tablespoon oregano
2 teaspoons salt
¼ teaspoon pepper
1 pound fresh mushrooms
1 medium eggplant
2 zucchini, ends trimmed

1. Heat the oil in a large, heavy saucepan or Dutch oven.
2. Add half the beef cubes and brown them on all sides over medium-high heat.
3. Remove the browned cubes; add the remaining beef and brown. Lift the browned meat from pan and set it aside.
4. Chop the onions and garlic medium-fine in the food processor or blender. Add them to the drippings in the pan and sauté 1 minute.
5. Return the beef to the pan, along with the tomatoes, oregano, salt and pepper. Break the tomatoes into chunks with a spoon.
6. Heat to boiling; then reduce heat, cover and simmer about 1½ hours or until the beef is tender, stirring occasionally.
7. Rinse the mushrooms and cut off the tips of the stem ends. Slice them.
8. Peel the eggplant. Cut it into pieces and slice it with a slicing blade.
9. Slice the zucchini with a slicing blade.
10. Add the mushrooms, eggplant and zucchini to the pan with the beef.
11. Cover and simmer 30 minutes or until the vegetables are tender, stirring occasionally.

Makes 8 servings

Vegetables

Vegetables prepared with a multipurpose machine or a food processor turn into Epicurean delights. For instance, the simple potato can be shredded into crispy Potato Pancakes and spinach haters will be converted to spinach fans when they sample the creamy, mellow Spinach Custard.

Spinach Custard

Mushroom Soufflé

Invite friends who have a passion for mushrooms and send them into raptures with a Mushroom Soufflé. This recipe uses a 1½-quart soufflé dish or other straight-sided baking dish. Because of the amount of mushrooms used, the soufflé will not tower above the baking dish like other, lighter soufflés. The recipe directions call for the mushrooms to be sliced in the food processor or with the slicing attachment of a multipurpose machine. The egg yolks and egg whites should be beaten separately in an electric mixer, not in the food processor, for maximum volume. The photographed directions show the recipe made with a KitchenAid K5-A.

  1 pound fresh mushrooms
 ½ cup butter, divided
  2 tablespoons lemon juice
 ¼ cup all-purpose flour
 ½ teaspoon salt
  1 cup milk
  4 eggs, separated
 ¼ teaspoon cream of tartar

1. Wash the mushrooms and trim the ends off the stems.
2. Slice the mushrooms in the food processor or with the slicing attachment of a multipurpose machine.
3. Melt ¼ cup of the butter in a skillet. Add the mushrooms and sauté until they are tender.
4. When sautéed, sprinkle the mushrooms with the lemon juice and set them aside in the skillet.
5. Melt the remaining ¼ cup butter in a saucepan. Add the flour and salt; cook and stir over medium heat.
6. Gradually add the milk; cook and stir until smooth and thick to make a cream sauce.
7. Stir the cream sauce into the mushrooms and keep them warm in the skillet.
8. Beat the egg yolks at high speed in a mixer until they are thick and lemon colored, about 5 minutes.
9. Blend a little of the hot mushroom mixture into the yolks. Add the yolk mixture to the mushrooms in the skillet and blend.
10. Wash the beaters. Beat the egg whites with the cream of tartar until stiff but not dry. Fold the yolk and mushroom mixture into the egg whites.
11. Turn the mixture into a 1½-quart soufflé dish or other straight-sided baking dish. Use a rubber or metal spatula to make a 1-inch deep ring in the surface of the soufflé — the ring forms a "top hat" as it bakes.
12. Bake in a preheated 350°F oven 30 to 40 minutes until delicately browned and the soufflé shakes only slightly when the oven rack is gently moved. Serve the soufflé immediately.

Makes 3 to 4 servings

Wash the mushrooms and trim the ends off the stems. Slice the mushrooms using the slicing attachment of a multipurpose machine, like the KitchenAid K5-A shown.

Melt ¼ cup of the butter in a skillet, add the sliced mushrooms and sauté until they are tender. When sautéed, sprinkle them with the lemon juice and set them aside in the skillet.

Melt the remaining ¼ cup butter in a saucepan and add the flour and salt. Cook and stir over medium heat. This mixture is known as a roux. Gradually add the milk and cook and stir over medium heat until smooth and thick — and *voila!* a cream sauce to stir into the mushrooms. Keep the mushroom-cream sauce combination warm in the skillet.

Using the high speed of the electric mixer, beat the egg yolks until they are thick and lemon colored, about 5 minutes.

Stir a small amount of the hot mushroom mixture into the egg yolks to temper or warm them up.

Now stir the egg yolks into the mushroom-cream sauce combination in the skillet.

Wash the beaters or whip of the electric mixer; then beat the egg whites with the cream of tartar until the whites are stiff but not dry. The whites are beaten enough if they do not slip when the bowl is tilted slightly.

Gently fold the yolk-mushroom mixture into the beaten whites.

Turn the mixture into a 1½-quart soufflé dish or other straight-sided baking dish. Using a rubber or metal spatula, make a ring about 1 inch deep in the surface of the soufflé — the ring forms a "top hat" as the soufflé bakes. Bake it in a preheated 350°F oven 30 to 40 minutes, or until the soufflé is delicately browned and jiggles only a little when the oven rack is gently moved. Serve the soufflé immediately.

Mushroom Soufflé

Potato Pancakes

Once upon a time, only a loving grandmother or special cook would hand-grate enough potatoes to make crisp, golden Potato Pancakes. Now, with a food processor or multipurpose machine fitted with a shredding attachment, the tiresome grating is eliminated and the beloved Potato Pancake takes only a few minutes to prepare. You can serve them with applesauce, if you wish.

3 medium potatoes, peeled
½ small onion, peeled
2 eggs
2 tablespoons flour
2 tablespoons milk
2 tablespoons butter, melted
½ teaspoon salt
Dash pepper

1. Shred the potatoes and onion; set them aside.
2. Mix the eggs, flour, milk, butter, salt and pepper using the plastic blade of the food processor or with the mixer of a multipurpose machine. Beat until blended.
3. Add the batter to the potatoes. Stir just until the potato shreds are coated.
4. Drop the batter from a ¼-cup measure onto a hot, greased griddle to make each pancake. Spread the batter to form 4-inch pancakes.
5. Brown the pancakes on one side; turn and brown the other side. Serve immediately.

Makes 8 pancakes

This recipe calls for two different blades in the food processor — the shredding blade for the chore of grating the potatoes and onion and the plastic blade for mixing the rest of the ingredients.

Shred the potatoes and onion with the shredding blade of the processor. Set them aside in a mixing bowl.

Mix the eggs, flour, milk, butter and seasonings, using the plastic blade of the processor. Beat until blended.

Add the batter to the potatoes and stir just to coat the potato shreds.

Using a ¼-cup measure, portion the batter onto a hot, greased griddle. Spread the batter with the bottom of a cup or spatula to flatten it into cakes.

Brown the pancakes until golden and crisp, then turn and brown the other side.

Potato Pancakes

Spinach Custard

With only a little more work than cooking the spinach you can have a mellow, impressive baked vegetable dish. Use the steel blade of the processor or blender of multipurpose machine to blend the ingredients.

1 pound spinach
1 carton (8 ounces) plain yogurt or
   1 cup dairy sour cream or 1
   package (8 ounces) cream
   cheese, cubed
3 eggs
1 small onion, peeled and
   quartered
½ teaspoon salt
½ teaspoon basil
   Dash pepper

1. Wash the spinach well. Place it in a saucepan, cover and cook it in only the water that clings to the leaves. Cook it for about 5 minutes or just until limp.
2. Combine the spinach with all the remaining ingredients in the food processor or blender and blend until smooth.
3. Pour the mixture into a buttered 1-quart baking dish or soufflé dish.
4. Bake in a preheated 325°F oven about 35 minutes or until a knife inserted near the center comes out clean.

Makes 6 servings

Roesti (Swiss Potatoes)

Shredded potatoes, Swiss cheese and onion are cooked in a frying pan until crisp and brown on the bottom. The shredding blade of a multipurpose machine or food processor will do the potatoes and cheese in an instant. The food processor's steel blade or a blender can handle the chopping.

4 medium potatoes
4 ounces Swiss cheese, chilled
1 medium onion, peeled and
   quartered
5 tablespoons butter, divided
1 teaspoon salt
   Dash white pepper

1. Cook the potatoes in their skins in boiling salted water until tender. Cool and peel.
2. Shred the potatoes and cheese with a shredding blade and toss lightly to mix.
3. Chop the onion finely in the food processor or blender.
4. Melt 3 tablespoons of the butter in a large skillet.
5. Add the onion and cook until tender, about 5 minutes.
6. Stir the onion into the potatoes along with the salt and pepper.
7. Add the remaining 2 tablespoons butter to the skillet and melt.
8. Spread the potatoes in the skillet, leaving enough space around the edge of the skillet so that you can check them as they brown.
9. Cook, uncovered, over medium-high heat about 5 minutes, or until the bottom is browned and crisp.
10. Turn the Roesti out onto a serving plate, with the browned side up.

Makes 4 to 6 servings

Garden Casserole

A summer cornucopia of fresh vegetables are combined in an attractive casserole. Use the vegetables listed in the ingredients or make up your own combinations, depending on what is ripe. Use the slicing blade of the food processor or multipurpose machine to cut even slices of vegetables.

2 medium carrots, peeled
½ pound green beans, ends
   trimmed
1 medium yellow squash, cut in
   short lengths
½ medium head cauliflower,
   separated into flowerets
1 medium zucchini, cut in short
   lengths
1 cup beef bouillon
1 teaspoon salt
½ teaspoon savory
½ teaspoon tarragon
3 tablespoons butter

1. Slice all the vegetables with a slicing blade and arrange them in layers in a buttered 1- or 1½-quart baking dish.
2. Heat the bouillon, seasonings and butter just to boiling in a small saucepan.
3. Pour the bouillon mixture over the vegetables.
4. Cover tightly and bake the casserole in a preheated 350°F oven about 30 minutes or until the vegetables are tender.

Makes 4 to 6 servings

Hot Mediterranean Potatoes

A savory vegetable dish that tastes twice as rich as it is, Hot Mediterranean Potatoes combines eggplant and potatoes. If you own a multipurpose machine with a potato peeler, let it peel the potatoes. A food processor can chop the potatoes, or they can be chopped by hand. The slicing blade of either kind of machine can be used to slice the onion.

2 large potatoes
¼ pound bacon, cut in 1-inch pieces
1 onion, peeled and quartered
½ clove garlic
2 cups peeled, cubed eggplant
¼ cup oil
3 tablespoons tarragon vinegar
1 tablespoon Dijon mustard
2 tablespoons grated Parmesan cheese
½ teaspoon salt
¼ teaspoon pepper

1. Peel the potatoes by hand or with a peeler attachment. Quarter and cook the potatoes in boiling salted water to cover until just tender.
2. Coarsely chop the potatoes in the food processor or by hand. Set them aside.
3. Cook the bacon in a large skillet until it is crisp. Remove the bacon and reserve the drippings.
4. Slice the onion and garlic with a slicing blade.
5. Sauté the onion, garlic and eggplant in the bacon drippings and oil until tender.
6. Gently stir in the potatoes.
7. Blend the vinegar and mustard. Sprinkle them over the potato mixture, along with the Parmesan cheese and seasonings.

Makes 4 servings

Peppers Romano

Easy to fix, robust in flavor, this vegetable is perfect with broiled steak, chops or fish. Use the slicing blade of the food processor or multipurpose machine to slice the peppers. The tomatoes can be sliced by hand or with the slicing blade.

3 or 4 large green peppers, seeded and quartered
2 cloves garlic
4 medium tomatoes, peeled
¼ cup olive oil
½ teaspoon basil or oregano
½ teaspoon salt

1. Slice the peppers with a slicing blade. Set them aside.
2. Slice the garlic. Set them aside.
3. Slice the tomatoes. Set them aside.
4. Heat the olive oil in a large skillet. Add the garlic and sauté until tender.
5. Add the peppers and sauté about 3 to 5 minutes.
6. Add the tomatoes and seasonings and simmer another 10 minutes.

Makes 6 servings

Winter Squash Casserole

Hard-shelled, winter squash comes in a variety of shapes and sizes — acorn, Hubbard, banana, buttercup and turban. But, no matter how peculiar its shape or name, the winter squash of your choice will look elegant in this delicious casserole. The few ingredients are quickly combined with the help of a multipurpose machine's blender or food processor's steel blade.

4 pounds winter squash
¼ cup pecans
¼ cup butter, divided
2 tablespoons packed brown sugar, divided
1 (1-inch) strip orange peel
½ teaspoon salt
⅓ cup raisins
1 tablespoon light corn syrup

1. Cut the squash in half lengthwise, or into medium-sized chunks.
2. Remove the seeds. Place the cut-side down on a baking sheet.
3. Bake in a preheated 400°F oven until tender, about 45 minutes.
4. Meanwhile, chop the pecans in the food processor (steel blade) or blender. Set them aside.
5. When the squash cools enough to be handled, scoop out the pulp.
6. Place half of the squash in the food processor or blender and purée.
7. Add the remaining squash and purée.
8. Add 3 tablespoons of the butter, 1 tablespoon of the sugar, the orange peel and salt. Blend until combined and the peel is grated.
9. Place the squash mixture in a 1½-quart casserole.
10. Stir in the raisins and half of the reserved pecans.
11. Combine the remaining butter, the remaining sugar and corn syrup in the food processor or blender. Blend until well combined.
12. Drizzle the syrup mixture over the squash.
13. Sprinkle the casserole with the remaining pecans.
14. Bake in a preheated 350°F oven 25 minutes.

Makes 6 servings

Vegetables

Crowned Sweet Potatoes

This recipe is like a vegetable "sundae." The puréed sweet potatoes are mounded in a cone shape and two delicious toppings are spooned over it. The combination of Spiced Cranberry Sauce and Creamy Lemon Sauce makes the sweet potatoes a perfect partner for the traditional holiday turkey or ham. The food processor's steel blade or a blender can purée the sweet potatoes quickly and can prepare the sauces.

3 large sweet potatoes or yams
¼ cup sherry or milk
¼ cup butter, softened
2 tablespoons brown sugar
1 teaspoon salt
Creamy Lemon Sauce
Spiced Cranberry Sauce

1. Cook the sweet potatoes in boiling salted water until tender. Peel and cut them into chunks.
2. Purée the hot sweet potatoes in the food processor (steel blade) or blender.
3. Add the sherry, butter, brown sugar and salt and blend until smooth.
4. Mound the potatoes in a cone shape on a serving platter or dish. Cover and keep them warm.
5. Prepare Creamy Lemon Sauce and Spiced Cranberry Sauce.
6. Alternately spoon the sauces over the sweet potatoes. Serve immediately.

Makes 6 servings

Creamy Lemon Sauce

1 onion slice (½-inch thick)
2 eggs
1 tablespoon lemon juice
⅓ cup butter
⅓ cup hot water

1. Purée the onion slice in the food processor (steel blade) or blender.
2. Add the eggs, lemon juice and butter. Blend until smooth.
3. With the motor running, add the hot water a little at a time until blended.
4. Turn the sauce into a saucepan. Cook and stir over low heat until smooth and thickened.

Makes about 1 cup

Spiced Cranberry Sauce

1 can (16 ounces) whole cranberry sauce
Thin outer portion of peel of ¼ orange
1 teaspoon cinnamon

1. Purée all the ingredients in the food processor (steel blade) or blender.
2. Turn the sauce into a saucepan and heat, but do not boil.

Makes about 1 cup

Zucchini Sauté

Guaranteed to convert squash-haters into squash fans, this simple recipe can be made in a twinkling with the slicing blade of any machine.

3 medium zucchini
1 small onion, peeled and quartered
3 slices bacon, chopped
1 teaspoon salt
Dash pepper

1. Slice the zucchini with a slicing blade and set them aside.
2. Slice the onion and set it aside.
3. Cook the bacon until crisp in a skillet or large saucepan.
4. Add the onion and sauté until tender.
5. Stir in the zucchini slices, salt and pepper, and sauté about 5 minutes or until tender.

Makes 4 to 6 servings

Cheese Topped Potatoes

Celebrate the arrival of spring with this recipe for new potatoes topped with a rich cheese sauce. The shredding blade of the food processor or multipurpose machine makes quick work of the cheese. If you have a potato peeler attachment for your multipurpose machine, let it peel the potatoes.

12 small whole new potatoes
4 ounces Gouda cheese, chilled
1 ounce Parmesan cheese, chilled
¼ cup butter
3 tablespoons flour
1½ cups light cream or half-and-half
¼ teaspoon dry mustard
¼ teaspoon salt
⅛ teaspoon white pepper

1. Peel the potatoes with the potato peeler of a multipurpose machine or by hand. Cook them in boiling, salted water until tender. Drain and keep them warm on a serving platter.
2. Shred the cheeses with a shredding blade. Set them aside.
3. Melt the butter in a saucepan. Blend in the flour and cook and stir until bubbly. Gradually add the cream. Cook over medium heat until thickened and smooth. Stir in the cheeses, dry mustard, salt and pepper until cheese is melted and thoroughly blended.
4. Pour the cheese sauce over the potatoes to serve.

Makes 4 servings

Sweet-Sour Carrots

Piquant flavored Sweet-Sour Carrots are superb served with pork chops or roast pork. The slicing blade of a multipurpose machine or food processor can prepare the vegetables in no time.

1 pound carrots, cut in short
    lengths
1 can (8 ounces) pineapple chunks
    in syrup
1 can (5 ounces) water chestnuts,
    drained
1 green pepper, halved and
    seeded
1 small onion, peeled and
    quartered
1 tablespoon cornstarch
1 tablespoon soy sauce
1 tablespoon vinegar

1. Slice the carrots with a slicing blade. Put them in a medium-sized saucepan.
2. Drain the pineapple, reserving the syrup. Add water to the syrup to make 1 cup.
3. Add the syrup-water to the carrots, cover and simmer about 5 to 10 minutes or until just tender.
4. Meanwhile, slice the water chestnuts, green pepper and onion and set them aside.
5. Blend the cornstarch, soy sauce and vinegar and add them to the carrots along with the sliced vegetables and pineapple chunks.
6. Heat to boiling, stirring occasionally, until the liquid is thickened.

Makes 6 to 8 servings

Sweet-Sour Carrots

Spinach Soufflé

The secret to a high-rising vegetable soufflé is in finely chopping the vegetables. Your blender or food processor's steel blade accomplishes this easily. However, do use a mixer to beat the egg whites for proper aeration. With special touches like a dusting of Parmesan cheese and a hard-cooked egg garnish, this soufflé is spectacular!

1 ounce Parmesan cheese, chilled
2 hard-cooked eggs, sliced
1 pound fresh spinach
2 ounces Swiss cheese, chilled
1 onion slice (½-inch thick)
2 tablespoons butter
2 tablespoons flour
½ teaspoon seasoned salt
1 cup milk
6 eggs, separated
¼ teaspoon cream of tartar

1. Grate the Parmesan cheese in the food processor (steel blade) or blender.
2. Butter a 2½-quart soufflé dish or casserole and dust it with the Parmesan.
3. Stand the egg slices upright around the side of the dish. Set it aside.
4. Wash the spinach well. Place it in a saucepan, cover and cook it in just the water clinging to the leaves. Cook until limp, about 5 minutes. Drain well.
5. Meanwhile, shred the Swiss cheese using a shredding blade and set it aside.
6. Chop the onion with the food processor's steel blade or in a blender.
7. Sauté the onion in the butter in a medium-sized saucepan.
8. Blend in the flour and seasoned salt. Cook, and stir until smooth and bubbly.
9. Stir in the milk all at once. Cook and stir until the mixture comes to a boil and is smooth and thickened. Remove the saucepan from the heat.
10. Add the shredded Swiss cheese; stir until it melts. Set the saucepan aside.
11. Beat the egg yolks in the food processor (plastic blade) or blender container until thick and lemon-colored.
12. Add the drained spinach. Turn the motor on and off quickly just until the spinach is finely chopped.
13. Stir the spinach mixture into the reserved cheese sauce. Set it aside.
14. In a mixer, beat the egg whites and cream of tartar until stiff but not dry; beat just until the whites no longer slip when the bowl is tilted.
15. Gently fold the spinach-sauce mixture into the whites.
16. Pour the spinach-egg white mixture into the cheese-dusted dish.
17. Make a ring about 1-inch deep and about 1 inch from the side of dish with a spoon or spatula.
18. Bake the soufflé in a preheated 350°F oven 30 to 40 minutes or until it is puffy and delicately browned; when done the soufflé should shake only slightly when the oven rack is gently moved back and forth. Serve it immediately.

Makes 6 servings

Mediterranean Mélange

Reap a harvest of flavor with this colorful vegetable medley. You will find it a breeze to prepare, even at the last minute, with a slicing blade and a multipurpose machine's blender or food processor's steel blade.

1 to 2 ounces Parmesan cheese, chilled
2 small-to-medium zucchini
1 green pepper, seeded and quartered
1 onion slice (1-inch thick)
2 tablespoons butter
2 medium tomatoes, cut in wedges
¼ teaspoon marjoram leaves, crushed
¼ teaspoon seasoned salt

1. Grate the Parmesan cheese in the food processor (steel blade) or blender. Set it aside.
2. Slice the zucchini with the slicing blade.
3. Cook the zucchini in just enough boiling water to cover until tender, about 5 minutes. Drain.
4. Meanwhile, place the green pepper and onion in the food processor or blender. Turn the motor on and off quickly just until the vegetables are coarsely chopped.
5. Sauté the chopped pepper and onion in the butter in a skillet until tender.
6. Stir the drained zucchini, tomatoes, marjoram and seasoned salt into the green pepper mixture.
7. Heat to serving temperature and drain.
8. Sprinkle with the reserved grated cheese to serve.

Makes 6 servings

Creamy Whipped Potatoes

Not just ordinary mashed potatoes! Spiked with just a little onion and enriched with sour cream, these whipped potatoes are magnificent. The food processor's steel blade or a multipurpose machine's blender can chop the onion. Turn to a mixer to whip the potatoes. If you have a machine with a potato peeler, here is a good place to use it.

6 medium potatoes
1 small onion, peeled and quartered
½ cup butter
⅓ cup hot milk
½ cup dairy sour cream
Salt
Pepper
Paprika

1. Peel the potatoes with the peeler attachment of a multipurpose machine or by hand. Cook the potaotes in boiling, salted water until tender. Drain and keep them warm.
2. Chop the onion finely in the food processor or blender.
3. Sauté the onion in the butter until soft.
4. Whip the hot potatoes in a mixer bowl. (If your mixer has a paddle or whisk, use it to whip the potatoes.) Gradually add the hot milk and butter-onion mixture. Stir in the sour cream. Salt and pepper to taste.
5. Pile the potatoes high on a heated serving dish. Sprinkle with paprika.

Makes 4 to 6 servings

Carrot Parsnip Tart

An early American favorite, Martha Washington probably served George a tasty pie like this. Of course, it took her a lot longer to prepare because she had to chop the vegetables by hand. You can chop them quickly with the steel blade of the food processor or in the blender of a multipurpose machine.

4 or 5 medium carrots, peeled and cut in chunks
1 small parsnip, peeled and cut in chunks
1½ teaspoons salt, divided
1 slice dry bread, torn in pieces
3 eggs
3 tablespoons butter
2 tablespoons lemon juice
1 tablespoon sugar
Dash white pepper
8-inch pastry shell
2 to 3 sprigs parsley

1. Cut off a few slices of carrot and parsnip and reserve them for garnish. Coarsely chop the carrots and parsnip in the food processor (steel blade) or blender.
2. Put them in a medium-sized saucepan with just enough water to cover. Add 1 teaspoon of the salt, cover and simmer about 25 minutes or until tender. Drain.
3. Make bread crumbs with the bread in the food processor (steel blade) or blender.
4. Add the cooked vegetables, eggs, the remaining ½ teaspoon of salt and all the remaining ingredients, except the pastry shell, to the bread crumbs and blend until smooth.
5. Pour the mixture into the pastry shell and bake in a preheated 375°F oven about 30 minutes or until a knife inserted near the center comes out clean.
6. Garnish the pie with the reserved carrot and parsnip slices and parsley.

Makes 6 servings

Carrot Parsnip Tart

Breads

The aroma of a piping hot loaf of Brioche can melt the heart of the severest kitchen critic. Brioche is only one of the delights in this chapter. There is a Lemon Loaf saturated with piquant sauce and a Zucchini Tea Loaf that is moist and tender beyond compare.

Blueberry Hill Bread

Lemon Loaf

A piquant-tasting quick bread, Lemon Loaf is the perfect accompaniment to your favorite blend of tea. Lemon Loaf gets its extra moistness from a drenching in lemon syrup after it has baked.

1 cup walnuts
1 lemon
1 cup sugar
½ cup butter, cut in chunks
2 cups all-purpose flour
½ teaspoon salt
2 teaspoons baking powder
1 teaspoon baking soda
¾ cup buttermilk
¼ cup lemon juice
½ cup sugar

1. Chop the walnuts; set them aside.
2. Cut the thin, outer colored portion of peel from the lemon with a paring knife or vegetable peeler.
3. Put the peel in the processor or blender container with the 1 cup sugar and blend or process until grated.
4. Add the butter in chunks to the lemon-sugar mixture in the processor and cream until light and fluffy. On other machines, cream the butter and lemon-sugar in a mixing bowl until light and fluffy.
5. Stir together the flour, salt, baking powder and soda.
6. Add half the flour mixture to the creamed mixture; blend or mix briefly. Add all of the buttermilk; blend or mix briefly. Add the remaining flour mixture and blend only until the flour is moistened. Do not overmix.
7. Stir in the nuts.
8. Turn the batter into a greased and floured 8½ x 4½-inch loaf pan. Bake in a preheated 375°F oven 1 hour or until a cake tester comes out clean.
9. Cool the loaf in the pan for 10 minutes before turning it out on a rack to cool.
10. While the loaf cools in the pan, stir the lemon juice and the ½ cup sugar together in a saucepan. Heat until the sugar dissolves.
11. Turn the loaf out of the pan onto a wire cooling rack set on a piece of waxed paper.
12. After the loaf has cooled, pierce its top thoroughly with a two-tined fork, cake tester, wooden pick or skewer. Slowly spoon the lemon-sugar syrup over the loaf so it can soak into the bread.
13. Let the loaf cool completely before slicing.

Makes 1 loaf

Chop the walnuts in the processor with the steel blade. Remove them from the container and set aside.

Breads

Cut the thin, outer colored portion of the lemon peel from the lemon and put it in the processor container with the sugar and process until the peel is grated.

Add the butter in chunks to the lemon-sugar mixture and cream until light and fluffy.

Stir together the flour, salt, baking powder and soda. Add half the flour mixture to the creamed mixture in the processor.

Add the buttermilk through the feed tube and blend just until combined. Add the remaining flour mixture and mix just until combined. Seconds count — so do not overmix!

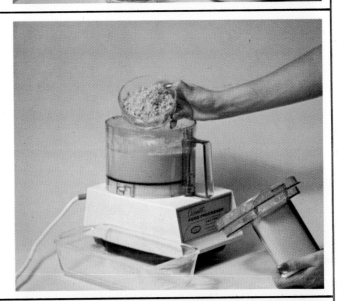

Add the nuts and stir until just until mixed.

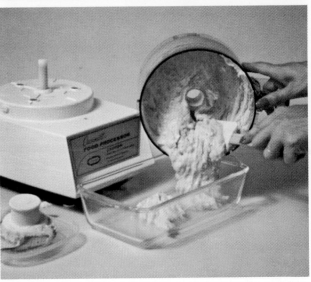

Turn the batter into a greased and floured 8½ x 4½ -inch loaf pan and bake in a preheated 375°F oven about 1 hour or until a cake tester comes out clean. Let the loaf cool in the pan while you heat the ½ cup sugar and the lemon juice in a saucepan until the sugar dissolves.

Cool the loaf on a wire rack set on a piece of wax paper. Pierce the cooled loaf with a cake tester, skewer, two-tined fork or wooden pick.

Spoon on lemon-sugar solution slowly and carefully, so the syrup soaks into the loaf. Let it cool completely before cutting.

Lemon Loaf

Brioche

A golden, eggy bread with a beautiful sheen to its crust, the classic Brioche has a topknot and is baked in a flared, fluted mold. You can make this recipe either with the steel blade of the processor or the paddle beater or dough hook of a multipurpose machine. You can form one large loaf or eight individual Brioche — tender and rich at any size. Brioche dough is often used to make Beef Wellington.

1 package active dry yeast
¼ cup water
1 tablespoon sugar
2 cups all-purpose flour
1 teaspoon salt
⅔ cup frozen butter, cut in chunks
2 eggs

1. Stir the yeast, water and sugar together in a small bowl. Let it stand while mixing the rest of the ingredients.
2. Put the flour, salt and butter in the processor or mixing bowl with a paddle beater or dough hook. Mix until crumbly.
3. Add the yeast mixture and mix until moistened.
4. Add the eggs and mix until the dough is smooth and begins to clean the sides of the bowl. If the dough appears to be too soft, add 1 tablespoon or more of flour.
5. Turn the dough out onto a lightly floured surface and knead until smooth, about 3 minutes.
6. Place the dough in a large, oiled bowl. Turn the dough to grease the top. Cover with a towel and let it rise in a warm place until doubled in bulk, about 1½ to 2 hours.
7. Punch the dough down.
8. To make one loaf, remove a small portion of the dough. Form it into a teardrop shape. Form the rest of the dough into a ball.
9. Place the large ball into a lightly oiled Brioche pan. Make a hole in center of the ball and insert the teardrop-shaped portion.
10. Cover and let rise until doubled, about 1 hour.
11. To make 8 small loaves, remove a quarter of the dough and shape it into 8 teardrop shapes and shape the remaining portion into 8 round balls. Follow the same procedure as for the large loaf, using small Brioche pans.
12. Bake the large loaf in a preheated 375°F oven for 45 minutes, or until golden brown. Bake the small individual loaves 20 to 25 minutes, or until golden brown.
13. Turn the Brioche out of the pan to cool on a wire rack before slicing.

*Makes 1 large loaf or
8 small individual loaves*

Whether you make 1 large impressive loaf, or 8 little ones, Brioche proves your skill as a breadmaker. The perfect Brioche has a distinctive golden crust and is tender and moist inside.

Breads

Stir together the yeast, water and sugar. Let the yeast mixture stand while mixing the remaining ingredients.

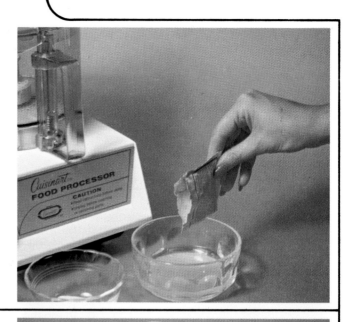

Put the flour, salt and chunks of frozen butter in the processor and mix until crumbly.

Add the yeast mixture and mix until moistened.

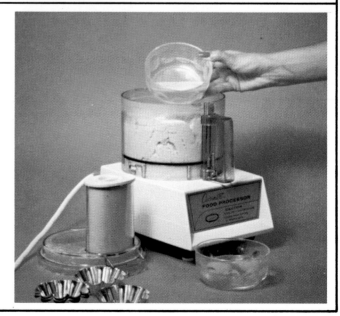

Add the 2 eggs and mix until dough is smooth and begins to pull away from the sides of the container.

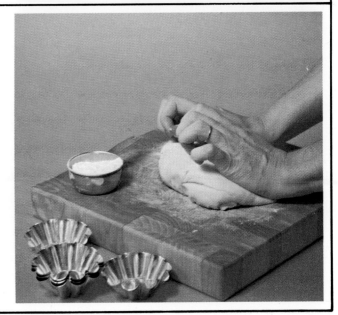

Turn the dough out onto a lightly floured surface.

Knead gently but firmly, pressing with the heels of your hands. Give the dough a quarter turn, knead, then give it another quarter turn. Repeat for about 3 minutes.

Put the dough into an oiled bowl, turning the dough to grease the top. Cover and let it rise until doubled.

The dough has doubled if, when poked gently with two fingers, indentations of your fingers remain.

Punch down the doubled dough. Turn it out of the bowl. Pinch off a piece of dough about the size of a golf ball and form it into a teardrop shape.

Place the large ball of dough in a lightly greased Brioche pan.

Poke a hole in the center of the large ball with your fingers.

Stick the narrow end of the teardrop shape into the hole in the large ball of dough.

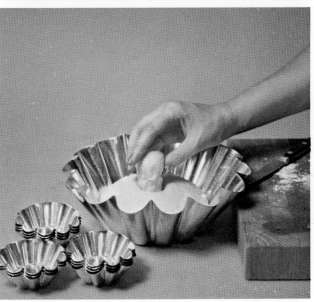

Cover and let the loaf rise in a warm place until doubled. Bake the large Brioche in a preheated 375°F oven for 45 minutes, or until golden brown. Turn the loaf out of the pan onto a wire rack to cool before cutting.

For individual Brioche, form 8 teardrop shapes and 8 small balls of dough. Put the balls in lightly greased, small Brioche pans.

Make holes in the centers of the dough in the pans and tuck in the teardrop shapes, small end first. Cover and let them rise in a warm place until doubled. Bake the small Brioche in a preheated 375°F oven for 20 to 25 minutes, or until golden brown. Turn the Brioche out of their pans to cool on a wire rack.

Brioche

Blueberry Hill Bread

Make several loaves of this delightful bread while blueberries are in season, then freeze them to enjoy later. Mixing is easy with the processor's steel blade or in the mixer of a multipurpose machine.

2 cups all-purpose flour
¾ cup packed brown sugar
2 teaspoons baking powder
1 teaspoon baking soda
1 teaspoon salt
½ teaspoon nutmeg
1 egg
¾ cup buttermilk or sour milk
3 tablespoons oil or melted butter
1 cup blueberries

1. Stir together the flour, brown sugar, baking powder, baking soda, salt and nutmeg in a small bowl.
2. Mix the egg, milk and oil in the food processor or mixer until well blended.
3. Add the dry ingredients and mix just until moistened.
4. Stir in the blueberries. (The batter will be stiff.)
5. Turn it into a greased 8½ x 4½-inch loaf pan.
6. Bake the loaf in a preheated 350°F oven 50 to 60 minutes.
7. Turn the loaf out of the pan and cool it on a wire rack.

Makes 1 loaf

Date Nut Loaf

This rich bread is a favorite for gift-giving. If you have a food processor, use its steel blade to chop the dates and nuts and blend the liquid ingredients. With a multipurpose machine, you can chop the dates in the blender or grinder; the liquid ingredients can be mixed in the blender.

2 cups all-purpose flour
1 teaspoon baking soda
1 teaspoon baking powder
1 package (8 ounces) pitted dates
1 cup packed light brown sugar
¾ cup pecans
1 cup water
1 egg
1 tablespoon oil

1. Stir together the flour, baking soda and baking powder in a large bowl.
2. Coarsely chop the dates, sugar and nuts. If you have a food processor use the steel blade. If you have a multipurpose machine chop them in the blender or in the grinder. Add them to the dry ingredients.
3. Blend the water, egg and oil in the food processor or blender.
4. Add them to the dates and dry ingredients. Stir until the flour is moistened.
5. Spoon the batter into a greased 8½ x 4½-inch loaf pan.
6. Bake the loaf in a preheated 325°F oven about 1 to 1½ hours or until done.
7. Turn the loaf out of the pan and cool it on a wire rack.

Makes 1 loaf

Rhubarb Bread

You will love this fragrant quick bread served warm or cold with whipped butter, cream cheese and, perhaps, some rhubarb jam. The rhubarb can be sliced with the slicing blade of any machine. Let the food processor's steel blade or a blender chop the nuts and grate the peel. The batter can be mixed — briefly — in the food processor or in a mixer.

½ orange
1 cup sugar
¾ pound fresh rhubarb, cut in short lengths
¾ cup walnuts
2 cups all-purpose flour
1 tablespoon baking powder
1 teaspoon salt
1 teaspoon cinnamon
1 cup milk
2 eggs
⅓ cup butter, melted

1. Cut off the thin, outer portion of the orange with a vegetable peeler or paring knife.
2. Grate the peel with the sugar in the food processor (steel blade) or in a blender. Set them aside.
3. Slice the rhubarb with a slicing blade.
4. Coarsely chop the walnuts in the food processor (steel blade) or in a blender, turning the motor on and off in short bursts. Set them aside.
5. Briefly mix the sugar-peel mixture, rhubarb, nuts, flour, baking powder, salt and cinnamon in the food processor or mixing bowl.
6. Add the milk, eggs and butter and mix only until moistened.
7. Turn the batter into a greased 9x5x3-inch loaf pan.
8. Bake the loaf in a preheated 350°F oven about 1 hour to 1 hour and 10 minutes.
9. Turn the loaf out of the pan and cool it on a wire rack.

Makes 1 loaf

Peanut Butter Bran Muffins

If some members of your family skip breakfast, consider baking these scrumptious muffins to hand them as they hurry out the door in the morning. You can mix them in only seconds with the food processor's steel blade or in the mixer of a multipurpose machine.

½ cup peanut butter
2 tablespoons butter
¼ cup packed brown sugar
1 egg
1 cup bran cereal
1 cup milk
¾ cup all-purpose flour
1 tablespoon baking powder
½ teaspoon salt
½ cup raisins

1. Cream the peanut butter, butter, sugar and egg in the food processor or with a mixer.
2. Add the cereal and milk and mix just until blended.
3. Stir together the flour, baking powder and salt. Add them to the food processor or mixer and mix only until the flour is moistened. Do not overmix.
4. Stir in the raisins just until mixed.
5. Spoon the batter into greased muffin pans and bake in a preheated 400°F oven 20 to 25 minutes.

Makes 1 dozen

Popovers

The characteristic shape of these crisp-crusted Popovers is created by the eggs in the recipe. Butter and preserves are the traditional popover accompaniments. The recipe can be prepared in the food processor with its plastic blade or in a multipurpose machine's blender.

2 eggs
1 cup milk
1 tablespoon oil
½ teaspoon salt
1 cup all-purpose flour

1. Place the eggs, milk, oil and salt in the food processor or blender. Turn the motor on and off quickly just until combined.
2. Add the flour. Process 20 seconds or blend 40 seconds.
3. Fill 11 greased popover cups or 11 6-ounce custard cups half full.
4. Bake the popovers on a baking sheet in a preheated 425°F oven 40 to 45 minutes or until brown and firm to the touch. For crisper popovers, prick the sides with a knife. Reduce the oven to 350°F and bake an additional 20 minutes.
5. Remove the popovers from the cups promptly. Serve hot with butter and preserves.

Makes 11 popovers

Peanut Butter Bran Muffins   **Popovers**

Breads

Almond Peach Bread

The heavenly aroma of this bread makes it irresistible, but if you can bear to wait. let the baked bread stand a day so the flavors can blend. The peaches can be puréed with the food processor's steel blade or in a blender.

     4 fresh peaches, peeled and pitted
    ½ cup water
 1¾ cups all-purpose flour
     1 cup sugar
     1 teaspoon baking soda
     1 teaspoon baking powder
    ½ teaspoon salt
    ½ teaspoon cinnamon
    ¼ teaspoon allspice
    ⅛ teaspoon cloves
     1 egg, beaten
     3 tablespoons butter, melted
     1 teaspoon vanilla extract
    ½ teaspoon almond extract
    ¾ cup pecans

1. Place the peaches and water in a saucepan; bring to boiling and cook 1 minute or until tender.
2. Pureé the peaches and water in the food processor (steel blade) or in a blender.
3. In a mixing bowl, stir together the flour, sugar, baking soda, baking powder, salt, cinnamon, allspice and cloves.
4. Combine the puréed peaches, egg, butter, vanilla, almond extract and pecans. Add them to the dry ingredients and stir only until moistened.
5. Pour the batter into a greased 8½x4½-inch loaf pan.
6. Bake the loaf in a preheated 350°F oven 45 minutes or until done.
7. Turn the loaf out of the pan and cool it on a wire rack.

Austrian Braid

Although it is especially nice at holidays, your family will appreciate this fragrant sweet bread at any time of the year. Use the processor's steel blade or the dough or paddle attachment of a multipurpose machine. The blender or food processor's steel blade simplifies lemon peel preparation, too.

    ½ lemon
 4½ to 5 cups all-purpose flour, divided
     2 packages yeast
    ½ cup milk
    ½ cup water
    ½ cup sugar
    ¼ cup butter
     2 teaspoons salt
     2 eggs
     1 cup golden raisins

1. Cut the thin, outer portion of peel from the lemon with a paring knife or vegetable peeler. Grate the peel in the food processor or blender. Set it aside.
2. Mix together 2 cups of the flour and yeast in the food processor or mixer bowl.
3. Heat the milk, water, sugar, butter and salt together in a saucepan over low heat until the butter melts and the mixture is very warm (120° to 130°F).
4. Add the liquid ingredients to the food processor or mixer bowl and blend about 30 to 45 seconds in the food processor or 3 minutes on the medium speed of the mixer.
5. Add the eggs, lemon peel and raisins along with 1 cup of the flour and beat until well combined.
6. Add enough of the remaining flour to make a moderately stiff dough. If using a food processor, add the flour a cup at a time, blend briefly, then add more. When the processor slows down, stop mixing.
7. Turn the dough out onto a lightly floured surface and knead until smooth and satiny, about 5 to 10 minutes. (Dough mixed in a food processor usually takes less kneading.)
8. Shape the dough into a ball and place it in a lightly greased bowl, turning to grease its top.
9. Cover and let it rise in a warm place until doubled, about 2 hours.
10. Punch down the dough and let it rest 10 minutes.
11. Divide the dough into 5 equal parts. Roll each part into a 20-inch long rope.
12. Braid three of the ropes together and arrange them on a greased baking sheet.
13. Twist the remaining 2 ropes together and put them on top of the braid.
14. Let the bread rise in a warm place until doubled, about 45 minutes. Bake in a preheated 350°F oven 35 to 45 minutes, covering loosely with foil if necessary, to prevent overbrowning.

Makes 1 loaf

Swiss Cheese Bread

The perfect beginning for a ham sandwich, Swiss Cheese Bread is delicious toasted. Use the shredding blade of any machine to prepare the cheese, then mix the bread in the food processor with the steel blade or with a dough hook or paddle attachment of a multipurpose machine.

8 ounces Swiss cheese, chilled
5½ to 6 cups all-purpose flour, divided
2 packages dry yeast
¾ cup milk
½ cup water
¼ cup oil
2 tablespoons sugar
2 teaspoons salt
1 to 2 teaspoons dried dill weed, optional
3 eggs, at room temperature
Butter, melted

1. Shred the cheese with a shredding blade and set it aside.
2. Mix together 2 cups of flour and the yeast in the food processor or mixer bowl.
3. Heat the milk, water, oil, sugar, salt and dill in a saucepan over low heat. Heat the pan until very warm (120° to 130°F).
4. Add the liquid ingredients to the food processor or mixer bowl. Blend about 30 to 45 seconds in the food processor or 3 minutes on medium speed in the mixer.
5. Add the eggs and cheese and blend until well-combined.
6. Add enough of the remaining flour to make a moderately soft dough. If using a processor, add the flour a cup at a time, blend briefly, then add more. When the processor slows down, stop mixing.
7. Turn the dough out onto a lightly floured surface and knead until smooth and satiny, about 5 to 10 minutes. (Dough mixed in the food processor usually takes less kneading time.)
8. Cover the dough with a bowl or a pan and let it rest 30 minutes.
9. Divide the dough in half and shape each half into a ball.
10. Put each ball in a greased, 1½-quart, round baking dish; turn the dough to grease its top.
11. Let it rise in a warm place until doubled, about 1 hour.
12. Bake in a preheated 375°F oven 25 to 30 minutes.
13. Remove the bread from the baking dishes to wire racks. Brush the tops with melted butter.

Makes 2 round loaves

Zucchini Tea Bread

Do not tell zucchini-haters the ingredients in this delicious, moist quick bread until after they have tried it. The zucchini can be shredded with the shredding blade of any machine. The food processor's steel blade or multipurpose machine's blender can be used to mix the liquid ingredients.

2 small zucchini
1 cup walnuts
3 cups all-purpose flour
1 tablespoon cinnamon
1 teaspoon baking soda
1 teaspoon salt
3 eggs
1½ cups sugar
1 cup oil
1 strip orange peel, 1-inch wide
1 strip lemon peel, 1-inch wide
1 tablespoon vanilla extract

1. Shred the zucchini with a shredding blade. Drain it well.
2. Place the nuts in the food processor or blender. Turn the motor on and off quickly just until the nuts are coarsely chopped. Set them aside.
3. Combine the flour, cinnamon, baking soda and salt and stir them into the drained zucchini.
4. Combine the remaining ingredients in the food processor or blender and beat until the peels are grated and the mixture is well-combined.
5. Pour the mixture in the food processor or blender into the zucchini mixture along with the nuts. Stir to mix.
6. Divide the batter evenly between 2 well-greased 9x5x3-inch loaf pans.
7. Bake the loaves in a preheated 350°F oven 60 minutes or until a wooden pick inserted in the center comes out clean.
8. Cool the loaves in the pans for 10 minutes before removing them to cool completely on wire racks.

Makes 2 loaves

Quick Bread Ideas

Finely chopping ingredients to add flavor and color to breads is a snap with the food processor or blender. To your favorite fruit quick bread, try adding a piece or two of crystallized ginger to chop with the fruit, or grate any citrus peel to add sparkle.

Try shredding 4 ounces of natural Swiss or Cheddar cheese and stirring it into your favorite bread dough. The flavor is delicious and the bread toasts beautifully.

For an easy loaf of Banana Bread, cream ½ cup butter, 1 cup sugar and 2 eggs in the food processor or mixer. Add 3 medium-sized ripe bananas and mix until smooth. Alternately stir in 2 cups all-purpose flour, 1 teaspoon baking soda, and a dash salt with 1 cup butter or sour milk. Mix just until moistened. Bake in a well-greased 9x5x3-inch loaf pan in a preheated 350°F oven about 1 hour.

Desserts

Pineapple Cherry Cheesecake

Cream Puffs

Cream Puff dough makes crispy holders for sinfully rich dessert fillings such as Almond Cream, included in the Dessert recipe section. The puffs are equally tasty filled with creamed hot dishes or cold salad mixtures. Use the steel blade of the processor or regular beater of a multipurpose machine for mixing the dough.

1 cup water
½ cup butter
¼ teaspoon salt
1 cup all-purpose flour
4 eggs

1. Combine the water, butter and salt in a saucepan and heat to a full rolling boil.
2. Remove the saucepan from the heat and stir in the flour all at once. Stir until the mixture forms a ball and pulls away from the sides of the pan.
3. Let the mixture stand 5 minutes, then turn it into the processor or mixing bowl of a multipurpose machine.
4. Add the eggs, one at a time, and process or mix well between each egg.
5. Drop the dough onto an ungreased baking sheet; use a scant ¼ cup or 2 tablespoons, placing each puff about 2 to 3 inches apart.
6. Bake in a preheated 400°F oven 35 to 40 minutes or until light golden brown.
7. Cool the puffs completely on a wire rack. Cut off the tops and pull out any filaments of soft dough. Fill with whatever filling you want.

Makes 12 puffs

It only takes five simple ingredients to create Cream Puffs. The eggs have to be beaten in one at a time and mixed well between each addition.

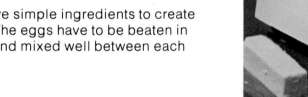

Combine the water, butter and salt in a saucepan and heat to boiling. Remove the saucepan from the heat and add the flour all at once.

Stir until the mixture forms a ball and pulls away from the sides of the pan.

Let the dough stand 5 minutes, then turn it into the processor. Add the eggs, one at a time, and mix well after each addition.

Drop the dough by 2 rounded tablespoons or scant ¼ cups onto an ungreased baking sheet. Bake in a preheated 400°F oven 35 to 40 minutes or until golden brown. Cool the puffs completely before cutting off their tops, pulling out any soft dough and filling them.

Cream Puffs Filled With Almond Cream

Orange Almond Cake

A delicate version of sponge cake, this dessert gets its flavor and texture from oranges, lemon and almonds. The food processor's steel blade or a blender does the chopping of the fruit and almonds. You can use the processor for all mixing or use the mixer of a multipurpose machine. Top this splendid dessert with whipped cream or fresh fruit, if you wish.

2 small seedless oranges
1 lemon
6 ounces almonds
6 eggs
½ teaspoon salt
1½ cups sugar
1 cup flour
2 teaspoons baking powder

1. Put the oranges and the lemon in a small saucepan and add water to cover. Heat to boiling, then reduce the heat, cover and simmer for 30 minutes. Drain and cool. (Save the juice to add to other recipes.)
2. Cut off the stem end of the oranges and lemon; cut the citrus in quarters and chop finely, but do not purée. Drain and set the fruit aside. (Save the juice for other uses.)
3. Chop the almonds until almost as fine as crumbs.
4. In the food processor or the bowl of a mixer, beat the eggs and salt until very thick and light — 1 minute in the processor, 5 minutes in the mixer.
5. Gradually add the sugar and beat until the sugar dissolves.
6. Stir together the flour and baking powder. Add them to the egg-sugar mixture in the food processor or mixing bowl. Mix until blended.
7. Fold the egg-sugar-flour mixture in a mixing bowl with the almonds and drained fruit. Fold them only until blended. Do not overmix.
8. Turn the batter into a buttered, 9-inch spring form pan.
9. Bake the cake in a preheated 350°F oven about 1 to 1¼ hours or until a knife inserted near the center comes out clean.
10. Cool the cake on a wire rack. Remove the sides of the pan when the cake is completely cool.

Makes one 9-inch cake

Organize and measure the ingredients for this light dessert. The key to making the cake as high and fluffy as possible is to avoid overmixing the batter.

Put the oranges and lemon in a saucepan and cover with water. Heat to boiling, then reduce the heat, cover and simmer for 30 minutes. Cut off the stem ends and cut the citrus in quarters.

Chop the quartered fruits in the food processor just until they are in fine pieces — do not purée them. Drain the fruit.

Put the almonds in the food processor.

Chop until they are almost the texture of crumbs.

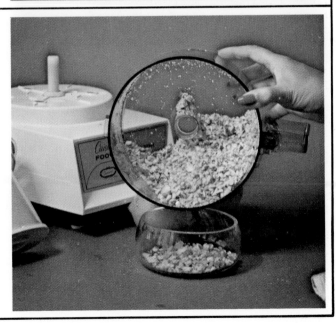

Beat the eggs and salt until very thick and light, about 1 minute in the food processor.

Gradually add the sugar and beat until the sugar dissolves. Stir together the flour and baking powder and add them to the egg-sugar mixture. Mix until blended.

Gently fold the egg-sugar-flour mixture in a mixing bowl with the almonds and drained fruit. Do not overmix.

Turn the batter into a 9-inch spring form pan and bake it in a preheated 350°F oven about 1 to 1¼ hours, or until a knife inserted near the center comes out clean.

Cool the cake on a wire rack. Remove the sides of the pan when the cake is completely cool.

Orange Almond Cake

Almond Cream Filling

Smooth and creamy with chunks of almonds, this filling for Cream Puffs is easy in a food processor with its steel blade or multipurpose machine's blender. After filling, Cream Puffs should be refrigerated.

¼ cup blanched almonds, toasted
½ cup sugar
3 tablespoons cornstarch or ⅓ cup all-purpose flour
¼ teaspoon salt
3 cups milk
3 egg yolks
1 teaspoon almond extract
¾ teaspoon vanilla extract

1. Place the almonds in the food processor or blender; turn the motor on and off quickly just until coarsely chopped. Set them aside.
2. Place sugar, cornstarch and salt in the food processor or blender. Turn the motor on and off quickly just until combined.
3. Add the milk and egg yolks. Blend until smooth. Pour the mixture into a medium-sized saucepan and cook and stir over medium heat until the mixture thickens and boils.
4. Boil and stir for 1 minute. Remove the saucepan from the heat.
5. Stir in the extracts and reserved chopped almonds.
6. Cover with plastic wrap and chill.

Makes 3½ to 4 cups

Cream Filling Variations
Coconut Cream Filling: In place of the almonds, shred 2 to 3 ounces fresh coconut. Omit the almond extract and increase the vanilla to 1 teaspoon. Proceed as for Almond Cream Filling.

Chocolate Cream Filling: Break 3 squares (3 ounces) unsweetened chocolate into a food processor or blender. Process until powdery. Continue with the recipe for Almond Cream Filling, omitting the almonds and almond extract and increasing vanilla extract to 1 teaspoon.

Lemon Cream Filling: Use only 2¾ cups milk. Omit the almonds, almond extract and vanilla. Grate the outer peel of 1 lemon, cut in strips, along with the sugar mixture. Proceed as for Almond Cream Filling, stirring in the juice of 1 lemon just before chilling.

Chocolate Topped Chocolate Mousse

A double chocolate treat, this elegant mousse is flavored with Grand Marnier. The mousse can be made with the food processor's steel blade or the blender of a multipurpose machine. The egg whites should be beaten with a mixer.

4 eggs, separated
¼ cup sugar
1 package (6 ounces) semi-sweet chocolate morsels or 6 ounces semi-sweet chocolate squares, cut in pieces
⅓ cup boiling hot strong coffee
½ pound butter, chilled and cut into chunks
¼ cup Grand Marnier
Dash salt
Chocolate Sauce

1. Beat the egg yolks and sugar until very thick in the bowl of a mixer or in a food processor, about 8 minutes. Set them aside.
2. Chop the chocolate in the food processor or blender.
3. Add the hot coffee and blend until the chocolate is melted, stopping the motor and scraping down the sides with a rubber spatula, if necessary.
4. With the motor running, add the butter a few pieces at a time; blend until the mixture is creamy smooth.
5. Add the chocolate to the egg yolk-sugar mixture, along with the Grand Marnier and salt. Blend until smooth. Pour the mixture into a large bowl.
6. Beat the egg whites with a mixer until stiff. Fold them into the chocolate mixture.
7. Pour the mousse into a 1-quart mold. Chill several hours or overnight.
8. Unmold it onto a serving dish. Spoon the Chocolate Sauce on top.

Makes 4 servings

Chocolate Sauce
1 cup milk
2 squares (2 ounces) unsweetened chocolate
Dash salt
¼ cup sugar
1½ teaspoons cornstarch
2 teaspoons water
½ teaspoon vanilla extract
¼ cup light cream or half-and-half

1. Heat the milk, chocolate and salt over low heat until the chocolate is melted.
2. Blend in the sugar and heat until the sugar dissolves.
3. Stir together the cornstrach and water. Add them to the chocolate; cook and stir until smooth and thickened.
4. Cool slightly. Stir in the vanilla extract and light cream.

Makes about 1½ cups

Key Lime Pie

A sweet-tart specialty from Florida, this pie is made with sweetened condensed milk. If you have ever scraped your finger grating citrus peel, you will appreciate the simplicity of grating peel in a food processor or blender.

2 to 3 medium limes or 4 small limes
⅓ cup sugar
3 eggs
1 can (14 ounces) sweetened condensed milk
9-inch crumb crust, chilled
Whipped cream, optional

1. Cut the thin, outer portion of the peel from the limes with a paring knife or vegetable peeler and put it into the processor or blender.
2. Cut off and discard the white portion of the peel. Quarter and seed the limes and add them to the peel along with the sugar.
3. Blend until the peel is finely grated and the mixture is smooth.
4. Add the eggs and beat until well blended.
5. Add the condensed milk and blend until smooth.
6. Turn into a chilled crumb crust and chill several hours or until firm.
7. Top with whipped cream, if you wish.

Makes 1 9-inch pie

Graham Cracker Crumb Crust

Preparing a crumb crust in a food processor or multipurpose machine is easier than taking the plastic cover off a commercially made crumb crust! Use the food processor's steel blade, or make cracker crumbs in the blender of a multipurpose machine.

22 to 24 square graham crackers
⅓ cup sugar
¼ to ⅓ cup butter, softened

1. Break the graham crackers into a food processor or blender and blend until crumbed. (In a blender, you will have to crumb a few crackers at a time, then empty them into a bowl to mix with the butter and sugar.)
2. Add the sugar and butter to the processor and blend until combined.
3. Put the crumb mixture into an 8- or 9-inch pie plate or pan and press firmly over the bottom and up the sides.
4. Bake in a preheated 350°F oven about 8 minutes or until browned. Cool completely before filling. The crust can be frozen or chilled until ready to fill.

Makes 1 8- or 9-inch crust

Note: For a vanilla wafer or chocolate cookie crust, crumb enough cookies to make 1⅔ cups crumbs and prepare as above.

Lime Cream Sherbet

Frozen desserts like this piquant sherbet can be prepared ahead and kept ready for planned or impromptu parties. The steel blade of the food processor or blender makes shredding the lime peel easy. The egg whites and whipping cream should be beaten with a mixer. Serve this zesty lime sherbet all year round as a light ending to a meal.

8 limes
1 cup sugar
2 cups milk
Green food coloring
2 egg whites
2 tablespoons sugar
1 cup whipping cream
Additional whipped cream, optional

1. Cut the thin, outer colored portion of the peel from the limes with a paring knife or vegetable peeler.
2. Grate the lime peel and 1 cup sugar in the food processor or blender.
3. Squeeze the juice from the limes.
4. Add the milk, lime juice, and a few drops green food coloring to the lime-sugar mixture in the food processor or blender; blend until smooth.
5. Pour the mixture into ice cube trays or a shallow pan. Freeze until firm, about 1½ hours.
6. Beat the egg whites with a mixer until frothy. Gradually add 2 tablespoons sugar and beat until stiff.
7. Whip the cream with a mixer until it is thick but not stiff.
8. Break the frozen mixture into chunks and beat in a processor or blender until smooth. Fold in the whipped cream and egg whites.
9. Spoon into 8 serving dishes or glasses. Place in the freezer compartment. Freeze until firm, about 2 hours.
10. If desired, garnish with additional whipped cream.

Makes 8 servings

Two-Tone Brownies

Sinfully rich and chocolaty, these brownies have a surprising white ripple of cream cheese. The whole recipe can be mixed in the food processor (steel blade) or the blender of a multipurpose machine.

1 cup butter, cut in chunks
2 cups plus 2 tablespoons sugar
4 eggs
¼ teaspoon salt
1 cup cocoa
1½ to 2 cups walnuts
1 cup all-purpose flour

Filling
1 package (8 ounces) cream cheese
⅓ cup sugar
1 egg
½ teaspoon vanilla

1. Blend the butter, the 2 cups plus 2 tablespoons sugar, the 4 eggs and the salt in the food processor or blender until light and fluffy.
2. Add the cocoa and nuts and blend just until the nuts are coarsely chopped.
3. Add the flour and mix just until moistened. Pour half of the batter into a greased 9x13x2-inch pan. Spoon out the remaining batter and set it aside. Wash the food processor or blender before making the cream cheese filling.
4. Put the cream cheese, the ⅓ cup sugar, the 1 egg and the vanilla in the food processor or blender and beat until smooth.
5. Spread the cream cheese mixture over the batter in the pan.
6. Spread the remaining chocolate batter over the cream cheese. Swirl slightly with a spatula or spoon.
7. Bake the brownies in a preheated 350°F oven 35 to 40 minutes.

Makes 18 brownies

Peanut Oatmeal Drops

Frosted with peanut butter frosting, these cookies will disappear just like salted peanuts. Fortunately, the recipe makes a large batch — about 5 dozen. The food processor's steel blade or a multipurpose machine's mixer can whip up the cookies in short order.

1 cup shortening
1½ cups packed brown sugar
2 eggs
2 cups all-purpose flour
2 teaspoons baking powder
1 cup quick cooking rolled oats
1 cup salted peanuts

Frosting
⅓ cup milk
½ cup peanut butter
3 cups powdered sugar

1. Measure the shortening, sugar and eggs into the food processor or mixer bowl and cream until light and fluffy.
2. Stir together the flour and baking powder and add them to the creamed mixture along with the oats and peanuts.
3. Blend or mix until combined.
4. Drop the dough by rounded teaspoonfuls onto lightly greased cookie sheets.
5. Bake in a preheated 375°F oven 10 to 12 minutes or until lightly browned around the edges.
6. Transfer the cookies to wire racks to cool.
7. For the frosting, combine the milk, peanut butter and powdered sugar in a food processor or mixer and blend until smooth. Frost the cookies when they are cool.

Makes about 5 dozen cookies

Two-Tone Brownies   Peanut Oatmeal Drops

Iced Blueberry Crème

When blueberries are in season, here is a glamorous, rich dessert that is easy to make. The blueberries can be puréed in a food processor (steel blade) or blender; use a mixer to whip the cream.

2 teaspoons unflavored gelatin
¼ cup cold water
1 cup fresh blueberries, washed and stemmed
2 cups whipping cream, divided
½ cup sugar
   Dash salt
3 tablespoons lemon juice

1. Sprinkle the gelatin over the cold water in a saucepan to soften.
2. Reserve a few blueberries for garnish. Purée the blueberries, 1 cup of the cream, the sugar and salt in a food processor (steel blade) or a blender.
3. Strain the puréed mixture into a large bowl.
4. Stir in the gelatin over low heat until dissolved. Add the lemon juice.
5. Stir the gelatin mixture into the blueberry-cream mixture.
6. Whip the remaining 1 cup whipping cream in a mixer bowl until thick but not stiff. Fold it into the blueberry mixture.
7. Pour the blueberry-whipped cream mixture into an ice cube tray or leave it in the bowl; freeze until mushy. Stir occasionally during the freezing process.
8. Spoon into dessert dishes while still soft. Garnish with the reserved blueberries.

Makes 6 to 8 servings

Brandied Cherry Sherbet

A sophisticated sherbet with a sweet-tart flavor, you can spoon it into pretty glasses to show off the lovely color. The sherbet can be mixed in a food processor (steel blade) or multipurpose machine's blender.

1 envelope unflavored gelatin
¼ cup cold water
1 package (1 pound) frozen red tart cherries
1½ cups water
½ cup cherry brandy or water
2 cups sugar
1 cup whipping cream
⅓ cup orange juice
2 tablespoons lemon juice

1. Sprinkle the gelatin over the ¼ cup cold water in a large bowl.
2. Heat the cherries, the 1½ cups water, and ½ cup cherry brandy in a saucepan until the cherries are thawed, about 5 to 8 minutes.
3. Blend the cherry mixture in a blender or food processor (steel blade) until smooth. Strain the mixture into a saucepan and heat to boiling.
4. Add the sugar and hot cherry mixture to the softened gelatin and stir until the sugar dissolves. Cool.
5. Stir in the whipping cream and fruit juices.
6. Pour the mixture into ice-cube trays or a shallow pan.
7. Freeze until mushy.
8. Beat the sherbet well in the food processor (steel blade) or blender. Then return it to the freezer.
9. Stir at least once or twice more during the freezing process.
10. To serve, spoon it into dessert dishes or glasses.

Makes about 1½ quarts

Magnificent Mocha Mousse

This dessert can be the crowning glory to your most spectacular meal. It is marvelously rich and has a hint of liqueur. The steel blade of the food processor or blender can chop the chocolate. A mixer should be used to beat the egg whites and whipping cream.

5 squares (1 ounce each) unsweetened chocolate
2 envelopes unflavored gelatin
¾ cup sugar, divided
½ cup very strong, very hot coffee
¼ cup coffee or chocolate liqueur
6 eggs, separated
½ teaspoon cream of tartar
2 cups whipping cream

1. Blend the chocolate in a food processor or blender along with the gelatin and ¼ cup of the sugar until finely chopped.
2. Add the hot coffee and blend until the chocolate melts and the gelatin and sugar dissolve.
3. Add the liqueur, mix and set aside.
4. Beat the egg yolks in a mixer or food processor (steel blade) until thick and lemon-colored, about 5 minutes. Gradually add ¼ cup of the sugar and beat until dissolved. Set it aside.
5. Beat the egg whites and the cream of tartar with a mixer until foamy. Add the remaining ¼ cup sugar and beat into stiff peaks.
6. Whip the cream with a mixer until stiff.
7. Fold the chocolate mixture, egg yolks, whites and whipped cream together just until blended.
8. Turn into an 8-cup mold and chill several hours or overnight.

Makes about 12 servings

Pineapple Cherry Cheesecake

Not too heavy, not to sweet, but just right! This lightly fruited cheesecake is bound to become one of your favorites. Use the steel blade of a food processor or a blender to save time and effort. You will need to whip the egg whites and whipping cream with a mixer.

Crumb Crust
- 18 zweiback, broken in chunks
- ⅓ cup sugar
- 2 teaspoons cinnamon
- ⅓ cup butter, melted

Filling
- 2 cans (8 ounces each) pineapple in pineapple juice
- 2 envelopes unflavored gelatin
- 3 eggs, separated
- ⅔ cup sugar
  - Dash salt
- ½ cup light cream or half-and-half
- 1 carton (16 ounces) small curd cottage cheese
- 1 lemon
- 1 cup whipping cream
- ½ cup maraschino cherries
  - Additional pineapple slices and maraschino cherries for garnish

1. Place the zweiback chunks into the blender or food processor along with the sugar and cinnamon; make crumbs.
2. Add the melted butter and mix well.
3. Pat the crumb mixture firmly over the bottom and about 2 inches up the sides of a 9-inch spring form pan. Chill.
4. Drain the pineapple, reserving the juice.
5. Sprinkle the gelatin over the pineapple juice to soften.
6. Combine the egg yolks, sugar and salt in a saucepan.
7. Gradually stir in the cream. Cook and stir over medium heat until the mixture coats a metal spoon.
8. Remove the saucepan from the heat and stir in the gelatin-pineapple juice mixture. Cover and refrigerate.
9. Put the cottage cheese in the processor or a blender.
10. Cut the thin, outer portion of peel from the lemon with a knife or vegetable peeler and add it to the cottage cheese.
11. Cut off and discard the white portion of the peel. Quarter and seed the lemon and add it to the cottage cheese.
12. Blend the cottage cheese mixture until the lemon peel is grated and the mixture is very smooth.
13. Add the cottage cheese mixture to the custard mixture and return them to the refrigerator until they begin to set.
14. Beat the egg whites until stiff in a mixer bowl.
15. Whip the cream with a mixer until stiff.
16. Coarsely chop the cherries in a blender or food processor.
17. Gently fold together the custard mixture, pineapple, cherries, egg whites and whipped cream.
18. Turn the filling into the crumb crust and chill several hours or until firm.
19. Garnish with additional pineapple slices and maraschino cherries.

Makes 10 servings

Frozen Peach Bowl Mousse

A dreamy dessert that enhances the summertime flavor of fresh peaches, this mousse can make your reputation as a hostess. The mousse should be prepared with a mixer, but the lemon peel can be grated in a food processor (steel blade) or blender. The slicing blade of any machine can slice the peaches quickly.

- 3 to 4 lemons
- 1 envelope unflavored gelatin
- 4 eggs, separated
- 1½ cups sugar
- 2 tablespoons orange-flavored liqueur (optional)
- 1½ cups whipping cream
- ¼ cup powdered sugar
- 1 pound fresh peaches, peeled, halved and pitted

1. Cut the thin, outer portion of the peel from the lemons and grate it in a food processor (steel blade) or blender.
2. Squeeze the juice from the lemons and measure ½ cup.
3. Sprinkle the gelatin over the lemon juice to soften. Set it aside.
4. Lightly beat the egg yolks in a medium-sized saucepan. Stir in the sugar, softened gelatin and lemon peel. Cook and stir over low heat until thickened.
5. Remove the saucepan from the heat. Stir in the liqueur.
6. Cool, then chill until syrupy.
7. Whip the cream and the powdered sugar with a mixer until thick but not stiff.
8. Beat the egg whites in a large mixer bowl until the whites no longer slip when the bowl is tilted.
9. Fold the whipped cream and chilled lemon mixture into the egg whites.
10. Slice the peaches with a slicing blade. Measure 2 cups of slices. Reserve the remaining slices for garnish.
11. Alternately spoon the mousse mixture and the 2 cups of peach slices into a 1-quart souffle dish or glass bowl, ending with the mousse mixture.
12. Cover the dish or bowl and freeze until firm.
13. One hour before serving, unmold the mousse on a serving plate.
14. Garnish with the remaining peach slices and refrigerate until serving time.

Makes 8 to 10 servings

Honey Mousse Tarts

Peaches and cream, sweetened with honey and enriched with eggs, are featured in this elegant dessert. For the mixing, use either a food processor (steel blade) or blender. For the slicing, use the slicing blade of any machine. The egg whites should be beaten with a mixer.

2 eggs, separated
¾ cup mild honey
Dash salt
1 cup whipping cream
4 fresh peaches, peeled, halved and pitted
8 (5-inch) tart shells, baked
¼ cup nuts

1. Beat the egg yolks and honey in a food processor or blender until smooth.
2. Pour the yolk-honey mixture into a small saucepan; cook and stir over low heat until slightly thickened, about 10 minutes. Pour into a small bowl, cover and cool.
3. Meanwhile, beat the egg whites and the salt with a mixer until the whites no longer slip when the bowl is tilted.
4. Whip the whipping cream with a mixer until thick but not stiff.
5. Fold the whipped cream and egg whites into the cooled honey mixture.
6. Slice the peaches with a slicing blade.
7. Arrange the slices in the tart shells, reserving several of the best slices for garnish.
8. Spoon the honey mousse into the tart shells. Freeze at least 1 hour or until the filling has the consistency of soft ice cream.
9. Chop the nuts in the food processor (steel blade) or blender. Use them to garnish the tarts along with the reserved peach slices.

Makes 8 tarts

Fresh Apricot Ice Cream

While fresh apricots are available you will want to make several batches of this splendid ice cream. Use the food processor's steel blade or a blender to purée the fruit.

2 pounds fresh apricots
1¼ cups sugar
2 cups light cream or half-and-half
2 cups whipping cream
1 cup milk
⅛ teaspoon salt
1 teaspoon vanilla extract

1. Dip the apricots a few at a time into boiling water for about 30 seconds. Plunge them into cold water and remove the skins.
2. Halve and pit the apricots.
3. Blend the apricots in a food processor or blender until smooth.
4. Combine the puréed apricots and the remaining ingredients in the container of a 4-quart electric or hand-churned ice cream maker.
5. Cover the container and place it in an ice cream maker; pack the ice cream maker with crushed ice and coarse salt, using about 1 cup salt per 3 quarts crushed ice.
6. Churn until frozen.
7. If the ice cream is not to be eaten immediately, repack it with fresh ice and salt or transfer it to a metal pan and place it in the freezer until serving time.

Makes about 2½ quarts

Frozen Peach Bowl Mousse And Honey Mousse Tarts

Fresh Apricot Ice Cream

Sauces Plus

Sauces, plus relishes, garnishes, beverages and other specialties that you can make in a twinkling with a multipurpose machine or a food processor appear in this chapter.

Lemon Curd

Hollandaise Sauce

Effortless and almost foolproof, this king of sauces takes only seconds to make in the processor with the plastic blade or in the blender attachment of a multipurpose machine.

3 egg yolks
2 tablespoons lemon juice
¼ teaspoon salt
   Dash paprika
   Dash cayenne pepper
½ cup butter

1. Put all the ingredients, except the butter, into the food processor or blender container and mix briefly.
2. Melt the butter just until it liquifies and begins to bubble.
3. Gradually add the butter to the processor or blender through the feed tube or opening in the top while the motor is running, mixing until smooth and thickened.
4. Serve the sauce at once. Any leftover sauce should be covered and refrigerated. Reheat the sauce over boiling water or by stirring in a very small amount of hot water.

Makes about ¾ cup

Lemon juice, egg yolks and butter, along with a few seasonings, form the basis of a rich and smooth Hollandaise Sauce.

Put the egg yolks, lemon juice, salt, paprika and cayenne in the food processor and mix briefly.

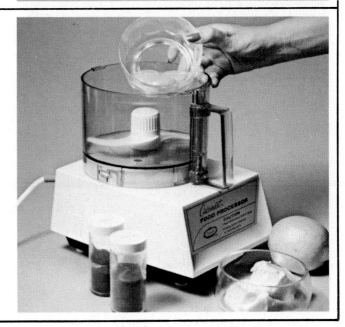

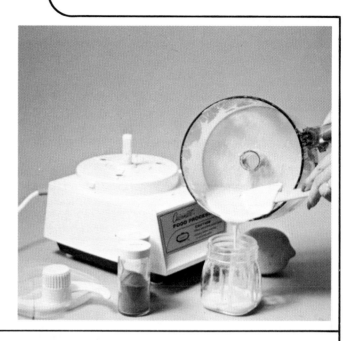

Add the melted butter gradually to the eggs with the processor running. If the sauce is not to be served immediately, pour it into a container and refrigerate until ready to use. Reheat over hot water or by stirring in a very small amount of hot water.

Bernaise Sauce

Adding a concentrated, seasoned vinegar blend to Hollandaise Sauce strengthens the sauce's flavor, making it especially good with meats.

¾ cup Hollandaise Sauce
2 tablespoons tarragon vinegar, white wine vinegar or white wine
¼ small onion, peeled
1 teaspoon dried tarragon
¼ teaspoon pepper

1. Prepare Hollandaise Sauce as the recipe directs.
2. Measure the vinegar into a small saucepan along with the onion, tarragon and pepper.
3. Simmer until the liquid is almost completely gone.
4. Add the vinegar mixture from the saucepan to the food processor or blender container and mix until smooth.
5. Serve the sauce at once. Cover and refrigerate any leftover sauce. Reheat it over boiling water or by stirring in a very small amount of hot water.

Makes about ¾ cup

A bit of onion, tarragon and tarragon vinegar or wine, simmered together to concentrate the flavors, turn Hollandaise Sauce into Bearnaise Sauce.

Add already prepared Hollandaise to the processor container, or prepare the Hollandaise Sauce recipe.

Simmer the vinegar, onion, tarragon and pepper until the liquid is almost gone, then add it to the processor and blend until smooth.

Serve the sauce immediately. Or, spoon it into a container and refrigerate until ready to serve. Reheat it over hot water or by stirring in a very small amount of hot water.

Mousseline or Chantilly Sauce

This variation of Hollandaise has whipped cream added and makes a rich but refined topping for vegetables, fish or chicken. Since the whipping cream is used more for flavoring and texture than for a high, fluffy volume, you can whip it in the food processor.

¼ cup chilled whipping cream, whipped
¾ cup Hollandaise Sauce

1. Gently fold the prepared Hollandaise Sauce into the whipping cream.
2. Spoon the sauce into a container to serve or chill the sauce until ready to serve.

Makes about 1¼ cups

Fold prepared Hollandaise Sauce into the whipped cream.

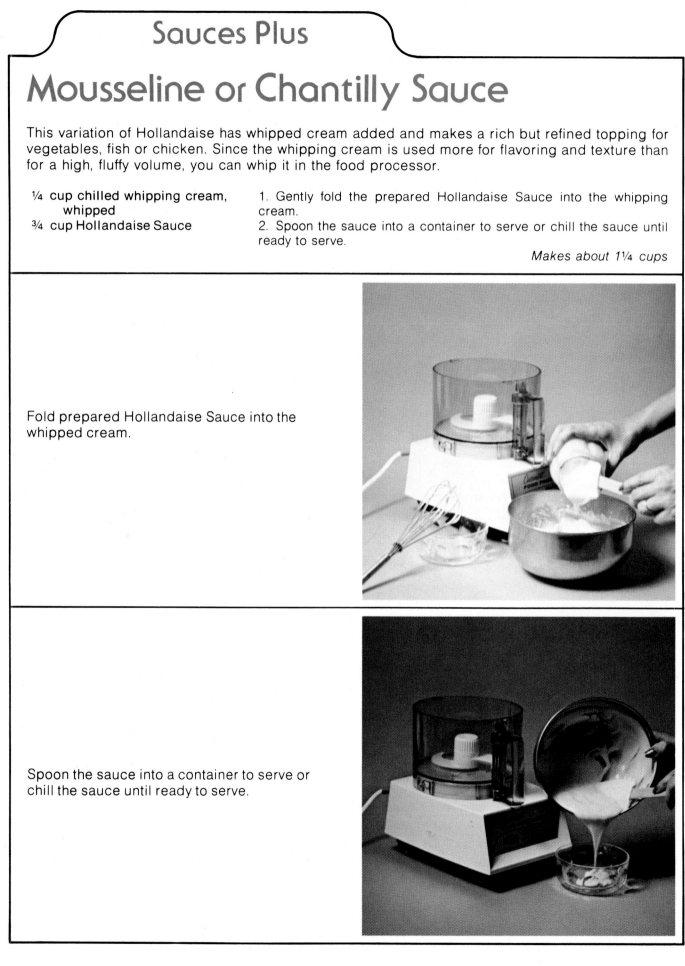

Spoon the sauce into a container to serve or chill the sauce until ready to serve.

Tomato Sauce

When the vines hang heavy with tomatoes, it is time to whip up a batch of this savory sauce. Try it over Moule au Fromage (Molded Cheese Loaf), over any *al dente* pasta, broiled beef patties or open face broiled cheese sandwiches. The chopping is easy with the food processor's steel blade or a blender.

1 medium carrot, cut in short lengths
1 medium onion, peeled and quartered
1 stalk celery, cut in short lengths
1 clove garlic
¼ cup butter
2 tablespoons flour
1 can (10½ ounces) beef bouillon
2 pounds ripe tomatoes, stemmed and quartered
2 or 3 sprigs parsley
¼ teaspoon sugar
¼ teaspoon thyme or marjoram
1 bay leaf

1. Finely chop the carrot, onion, celery and garlic in the food processor or blender.
2. Melt the butter in a large saucepan. Add the chopped vegetables and sauté over medium heat 5 to 10 minutes. Do not brown.
3. Blend in the flour and cook until bubbly.
4. Add the bouillon and cook and stir until the mixture comes to a boil and is smooth and thickened.
5. Chop the tomatoes in the food processor or blender and add them to the saucepan.
6. Chop the parsley and add it to the pan, along with the sugar and seasonings.
7. Simmer very slowly 1½ to 2 hours, stirring occasionally, until the sauce is thick.
8. Strain. If the sauce is not used at once, cover it tightly and refrigerate or freeze.

Makes about 2½ cups

Cheese Sauce

Easy to prepare, this rich sauce can complement many dishes. Choose any firm cheese compatible with the food to be enhanced. Use a shredding blade to handle the cheese.

2 ounces firm cheese (Swiss, Gruyere, Cheddar, Monterey Jack, etc.), chilled
2 tablespoons butter
2 tablespoons flour
1¼ teaspoons salt
Dash cayenne pepper
1 cup liquid (vegetable liquid, meat broth, milk or any combination)

1. Shred the cheese with a shredding blade. Set it aside.
2. Melt the butter in a saucepan.
3. Blend in the flour, salt and cayenne pepper.
4. Cook and stir until smooth and bubbly.
5. Stir in the liquid all at once. Heat to boiling, stirring constantly.
6. Boil and stir until the sauce is smooth and thickened.
7. Remove the saucepan from the heat.
8. Stir in the cheese until it has melted.

Makes about 1¼ cups

Creamed Mushrooms

Spooned over *al dente* pasta, rice, hot cooked asparagus or toast points, this sauce is rich and absolutely delicious! The slicing blade of the food processor or other machine can handle the mushrooms.

1 pound fresh mushrooms
2 tablespoons butter
1 tablespoon lemon juice
1 tablespoon flour
¾ teaspoon salt
¼ teaspoon nutmeg
Dash white pepper
1 cup whipping cream

1. Rinse the mushrooms and cut off just the tips of the stem ends.
2. Slice the mushrooms with a slicing blade.
3. Melt the butter in a large skillet. Add the mushrooms and sauté until they are tender.
4. Sprinkle with the lemon juice, and then with the flour and seasonings; stir to mix.
5. Add the cream; cook and stir until the mixture is smooth and thick.
6. Serve at once.

Makes about 3 cups

Pesto

Pesto is a robust Italian topping for soup such as Minestrone, or it can be tossed with hot cooked pasta. Traditionally, Pesto required a mortar and pestle and a strong arm, but the food processor's steel blade or blender modernizes the preparation.

¼ cup butter
¼ cup grated Parmesan cheese
¼ cup olive oil
¼ cup walnuts or pine nuts
4 or 5 sprigs parsley
1 clove garlic
1 teaspoon basil

1. Combine all the ingredients in the food processor or blender and blend until finely chopped.

Makes about ¾ cup

Marinara Sauce

A thick, chunky, robust sauce, Marinara Sauce is delicious spooned over baked chicken, fish, meat, or over pasta cooked *al dente*. The recipe directions tell how to make the sauce in either the food processor or multipurpose machine.

4 medium onions
2 large green peppers
    seeded and quartered
2 cloves garlic
½ cup olive oil
5 pounds tomatoes
2 teaspoons salt
1 teaspoon rosemary
1 teaspoon thyme
1 teaspoon basil

1. Peel and slice the onions or chop them coarsely in the food processor or a blender container.
2. Slice or coarsely chop the green peppers.
3. Chop the garlic finely.
4. Heat the oil in a large pan; add the garlic and vegetables and sauté them until limp and tender, about 10 minutes.
5. Peel the tomatoes by dipping them briefly in boiling water to loosen the skins. Chop the tomatoes. Strain the tomatoes to remove the seeds, if desired.
6. Add the tomatoes to the pan along with the salt, rosemary, thyme and basil.
7. Simmer uncovered about 2 hours, or until thick.
8. Refrigerate any unused portion, or ladle the sauce into a freezer container and freeze. You can also pack the sauce into clean, hot pint jars. Seal and process the jars in a pressure canner at 10 pounds pressure for 45 minutes.

Makes about 5 pints

Marinara Sauce

Quick Garnish Ideas

A fanciful topping or garnish for almost any dish becomes second nature when you have a kitchen machine to chop, shred or slice for you. The following suggestions are just to get you started. You will soon be coming up with special toppings.

Chopping parsley used to be a laborious chore, but no more. Add just a smattering of the bright green flecks over any form of potatoes; sprinkle chopped parsley on soups, over open-face sandwiches, or on steaks, chops or fish.

Keep radishes on hand for pretty toppings for soups, salads or steaks. Sliced, shredded or coarsely chopped, they add bright color and just a spark of flavor. Scatter some slices over gravy in a gravy boat, toss some shreds into an ordinary tossed salad, float chopped radishes in clear broth.

Dutch Salad

This "salad" is really an old-fashioned relish that combines almost everything in the garden. Dutch Salad is delicious with meats and cold cuts. The recipe makes about 13 pints so you can have some jars for gift giving, too. The steel blade of the processor chops in seconds what ordinarily would take almost an hour. With multipurpose machines, use the slicing attachment or blender to handle the chopping chores. You will need standard pint or quart canning jars and lids, as well as a water bath canner.

1 head cauliflower, separated into flowerets
1 head cabbage (about 2 pounds), cut in chunks
1 bunch celery, cut in short lengths
2 pounds green tomatoes
4 medium onions, peeled and quartered
3 sweet red peppers, seeded
3 medium cucumbers, cut in short lengths
1 gallon water
1 cup pickling salt

The Second Day
3 cups sugar
1 cup flour
3 pints and 1 cup cider vinegar
1 pint water
2 tablespoons celery seed
2 tablespoons mustard seed
1 tablespoon tumeric

1. Leave the cauliflower in small flowerets, or slice or chop them coarsely. Put them in a large bowl or crock.
2. Slice or chop the cabbage coarsely. Add it to the bowl with the cauliflower.
3. Slice or chop the celery coarsely. Add it to the bowl.
4. Stem the green tomatoes and chop them coarsely and add them to the bowl.
5. Chop the onions, peppers and cucumbers coarsely and add them to the bowl.
6. Combine the 1 gallon water and the pickling salt and stir until the salt dissolves.
7. Pour the salt brine over the vegetables and let them stand overnight.
8. The next morning, drain the vegetables thoroughly.
9. Stir together the sugar and flour in a saucepan, then blend in the 1 cup cider vinegar and stir to a thick paste.
10. Put the sugar-flour mixture, the 3 pints of cider vinegar and all remaining ingredients in a large kettle and heat until boiling.
11. Add the drained vegetables; heat to boiling. Lower the heat and simmer 20 minutes, stirring frequently.
12. Ladle the relish into clean, hot pint jars to within ½ inch of each top.
13. Seal the jars following the lid manufacturer's directions.
14. Process in a boiling water bath for 20 minutes.

Makes about 13 pints

Lemon Curd

An English treat, Lemon Curd is a piquant spread for muffins or toast. It also makes a tasty filling for tart shells. The food processor's steel blade or the blender of a multipurpose machine is used to prepare the lemons.

2 lemons
1 cup sugar
Dash salt
3 eggs
½ cup butter

1. Cut the thin, outer portion of peel from the lemons with a paring knife or vegetable peeler.
2. Put the peel in the food processor (steel blade) or blender along with the sugar and process or blend until grated.
3. Squeeze the juice from the lemons and add it to the food processor or blender along with all the other ingredients. Process or blend until well combined.
4. Pour the mixture into a small saucepan. Cook and stir over medium heat just until it thickens.
5. Remove the saucepan from the heat and pour the Lemon Curd into a container. Cover and chill.

Makes about 1½ cups

Fresh California Chutney

Here is a spicy sweet chutney to keep on hand in the refrigerator. It can be mixed with mayonnaise for a spunky salad dressing, used as a basting sauce for barbecued chicken, stirred into hot rice pilaf, served with curries, or just enjoyed as a relish. The processor's steel blade or slicing blade, or the blender or slicing blade of a multipurpose machine simplifies the preparation. The chutney is not processed in a water bath and must be refrigerated.

½ cucumber,
2 green onions, cut in short
    lengths
1 apple, peeled, cored and
    quartered
2 cups cherry tomatoes, quartered
1 cup raisins
1 cup seedless grapes
1 teaspoon ground coriander
1 teaspoon salt
¼ teaspoon pepper
½ orange
1 jar (10 ounces) red currant jelly
1 teaspoon prepared horseradish

1. Chop or slice the cucumber, onions and apple.
2. Combine them with the tomatoes, raisins, grapes and seasonings in a large bowl.
3. Cut off the thin, outer portion of peel from the orange with a knife or vegetable peeler. Grate it in the food processor or blender.
4. Stir the grated peel into the fruit mixture.
5. Spoon the chutney into jars or other containers.
6. Heat the jelly and horseradish just until soft and stir until blended.
7. Spoon the jelly on top of the chutney in the containers. Cover and chill.

Makes about 7 cups

Calliope Cooler

For a special refreshing treat, try Calliope Cooler. The flavored and colored cubes of frozen milk make a unique addition to this version of iced café au lait. The recipe can be made with the food processor's steel blade or a blender.

5 cups milk, divided
1 tablespoon sugar
½ teaspoon vanilla
2 tablespoons strawberry jam
2 cups cold, strong coffee

1. Stir together 1½ cups of the milk, sugar and vanilla. Pour into an ice cube tray and freeze until firm.
2. Combine 1½ cups of the remaining milk with the jam in the food processor or blender and blend until smooth. Pour into an ice cube tray and freeze until firm.
3. To serve, alternate the white and pink cubes in large glasses or mugs.
4. Pour the remaining 2 cups milk and the coffee simultaneously into the mugs over the cubes.

Makes 4 servings

Spirited Strawberry Shake

Simple to make and delicious, this is a sophisticated milk shake. If the younger set wants to enjoy the shake, omit the kirsch. Prepare the shake in the food processor with the steel blade or in a blender.

1 cup milk
½ pint strawberry ice cream
6 to 8 strawberries, hulled
1 tablespoon kirsch

1. Combine all the ingredients in the food processor or blender and blend until smooth.
2. Pour into 2 chilled glasses.

Makes 2 servings

Quick Chocolate Fizz

An easy version of a chocolate soda, this fizz has a hint of orange in it. Use the food processor's steel blade or a blender to do the mixing.

2 cups milk
½ cup chocolate syrup
⅛ teaspoon orange extract
1 pint vanilla ice cream, divided
2 cups chilled club soda or
    sparkling water

1. Combine the milk, chocolate syrup, extract and 1 cup of the ice cream in the blender or food processor and blend until smooth.
2. Pour into 4 tall glasses, and top each with a small scoop of ice cream.
3. Fill the glasses with soda. Serve immediately.

Makes 4 servings

Test Reports

American Electric Food Processor 8000

This machine has direct drive, a top-operated on/off control, an automatic overload cutoff and braking action. Although it handled most processing tasks adequately in our tests, the American Electric Food Processor cut off frequently when processing heavy loads. It also "walked" around the counter during operation. We found the blades difficult to clean.

The American Electric Food Processor lacks the extra quality, easy use and smooth action demonstrated by other food processors we've tested. It is, however, one of the least expensive food processing machines on the market.

Cuisinart Food Processors CFP-5A/CFP-9

Though both Cuisinarts are quite compact, neither is a kitchen gadget to be purchased on impulse. The CFP-9 is about $30 cheaper than the CFP-5A, but both appliances are expensive. Slicing, shredding, chopping, grating, mixing and puréeing are efficiently done by changing blades inside their Lexan mixing containers, also called beakers. The sturdy beaker sits on top of the motor. The beaker is somewhat smaller than the mixing bowls on multipurpose mixers (approximately 6½ inches and 3¾ inches deep). The cover for the beaker has a feed tube that has two functions: it is a chute for food to be sliced or shredded; and it is a handle for rotating the cover in order to turn the motor on and off.

The CFP-5A has lock-in blades, a safety feature

Cuisinart® CFP-5A

lacking on the CFP-9 and earlier models. The lock-in blade feature means the steel blade cannot come out of position when processing heavy mixtures and liquids that rise above the center core cannot leak out.

The beaker on the CFP-5A has a handle. The CFP-9 lacks a handle on the bowl and has a plastic base rather than a metal one like the CFP-5A. The handle is an advantage when emptying the bowl. For around $4.00 you can buy a handle especially designed to attach to the CFP-9 or to replace a broken handle on the CFP-5A. CONSUMER GUIDE Magazine's home economists could tell no difference in performance between the CFP-5A and the less expensive CFP-9.

Both processors come with four blades: a steel blade for chopping, mixing and puréeing; a thick-slicer; a thick-shredder; and a plastic blade for mixing such items as sauces. You will probably use the chopping blade and slicing blade most frequently.

Additional blades are available for about $14.00 each. At that price you want to be sure the blade is something you will really use. There is a French-fry cutter that can cut any hard vegetable into French-fry shapes. Though it has limited uses, it is a nice addition if you like to deep-fry foods. The thin-slicer is an excellent addition. It makes very fine, even slices out of any hard to medium-hard vegetable. The thin-shredder is also a good addition. You can make fine-shredded cole slaw or thin-shredded potatoes for potato pancakes. It makes almost julienne-shaped shreds that could be used in salads. The ripple cutter is the most limited in use. It makes very thin, slightly wavy slices. We thought they were too thin for cooked or deep-fried vegetables. Ripple-cut cooked carrots lost their ripple and deep-fried, ripple-cut potatoes were too fragile to handle. However, the blade made pretty cucumbers for salad. Before buying any of these optional blades, consider your cooking habits and evaluate how often you would use the blade.

The most expensive attachment for the Cuisinart is the juice extractor. This device sits on top of the beaker with a feed tube for non-citrus fruits or vegetables. Once you figure out the rather obscure directions, very clear fruit and vegetable juices can be made easily with the extractor. It is easy to clean, too.

The pulp collects in the top, and there is a plastic ejection switch to empty the pulp. However, to avoid spilling the pulp, we recommend placing a bowl under the ejection spout for the pulp, or attaching a plastic bag to the spout with a rubber band. There is a large amount of pulp (fiber) for a small amount of juice. This is a specialty attachment with limited use. It is for those who really love carrot juice or other vegetable juices. Compared to the price of other juice extractors, the Cuisinart's attachment is reasonable. Again, it only extracts non-citrus juice; it will not squeeze an orange for you.

Cuisinart DLC7 Food Processor

The new machine is stronger, quieter, has a longer slicing blade, a new pulse switch and an on/off switch. The bowl capacity is 46% bigger than the other Cuisinart models, a real boon to bakers and cooks with families. This model can handle a 6-cup-flour batch of yeast dough (most other machines will tackle only 3-cup loads).

Another change from the other Cuisinart models, the feed tube can be positioned from the front or back of the machine. We prefer the front because of working under cabinets, but at least the choice is yours. The braking action on this Cuisinart is exceptional. The blades halt within a few seconds. This is, we think, a very important safety factor.

The DLC7 did a fine job on all our tests. Its quiet motor and efficient operation make it top-of-the-line, not only of Cuisinart's line but every line. And you pay for that quality, too—$250.00 is the suggested retail price.

The DLC7 has a one-year warranty on the entire machine, plus an exceptional 30-year warranty on the motor.

If a bigger bowl isn't important to you, then consider the smaller, less expensive Cuisinart models.

Cuisinart DLC-7

Farberware Food Processor 286

The Farberware Food Processor does not look exactly like the Cuisinart, though its basic functions are the same. The Farberware's belt-driven motor is in the back of the work bowl, rather than underneath it. As a result, it takes up more counterspace than many of the other machines. This design creates sort of a tray that the bowl sits in; this tray is not quite as easy to clean as some other food processors.

The Farberware stood up to all our tests and performed well for the most part. It was not able to handle as heavy a dough as either the CFP-5A or less expensive Cuisinart. Some food collected between the slicing and shredding blade and the cover. It lacks a handle on the bowl; it would be easier to empty if it had a handle.

In its favor, the Farberware has an extra bulge in the feed tube, so you can insert larger vegetables, fruits or pieces of food. This also means that there is only one way for the pusher to fit in place. On most other machines there is no front or back to the pusher, a small advantage when you are working quickly.

The use and care booklet has over 60 recipes, as well as adequate basic instructions.

GE Food Processor FP-1

GE's processor offers one reversible blade to handle both slicing and shredding, and a steel blade for chopping and mixing. The bowl and cover cannot be washed in the dishwasher, a disadvantage for many people, we think. The bowl does have a handy fill line, showing you just how far you can go. The post assembly is sealed with a rubber gasket, so there should not be any leaking from the bowl. There is a one-year warranty, detailed instructions for use and a handy "daily use" chart, along with specific and clear do's and don'ts. Among those don'ts are raw meat and soft or sticky products. Some of the heavier processors will handle these foods. You can use the knife and the slicing or shredding disc at the same time, a dubious feature we think, unless you are aiming for purées or an even quicker job of reducing something to extra fine pieces.

The GE processor cannot handle yeast doughs. It is very loud and walks across the counter when processing heavy loads. The instruction book recognizes this fact and directs you to hold it down while processing hard foods. It chops satisfactorily but does not slice or shred as well as many of the other processors. There is no braking action on the blades. The GE model does have two easy to work switches, an on-off switch and a pulse button. The bowl and cover are easy to put in place and use. But the noise, the movement and overall performance make it unacceptable, we think.

GE Food Processor Plus Blender FP-2

The GE Food Processor plus Blender FP-2 is a multi-purpose appliance. This machine is a combination of the modified food processor base and motor of the FP-1, and a blender container. The only advantage we found in the combination was that the opportunity to use one base for two functions saves counter space.

The FP-2 can slice, chop, shred, grate, grind and mince. The five-speed blender stirs, purées, blends, liquefies and crushes ice. A 160-page cookbook comes with the GE FP-2. It contains color illustrations and information on how to use every feature of the machine.

Hamilton Beach Food Processor 707

The first Hamilton Beach processor we tested looked promising, until we tried to get the bowl off the base to wash it. It would not come off at all. So we sent it back and got another one. The second one worked, and very well at that. The Hamilton Beach processor comes with shredding and slicing blades, as well as a metal knife blade and a plastic blade for mixing. It has a three position switch (on/off/pulse) and automatic cut-off. Its motor is belt driven. The accompanying instruction book is the best we have seen. Included in the booklet are good yield charts, clear explanations of what each blade should do, how and why, with valuable photos of food processor techniques. This processor has suction feet to keep it in place on the counter, although we did not notice any movement or jumping when it was operated.

Our only complaints, and small ones at that, were with the length of the cord (only 20 inches) and the horizontal action of the switch. We found that it was easy to push the switch too far when using the pulse cycle, thus turning the processor to the full "on" position. This was really a minor point, however. The Hamilton Beach machine did a good job in all our tests and a particularly nice job on yeast doughs.

Merit Food Processor FP-100

A heavyweight machine, Merit's processor is almost an exact look-alike and work-alike to the Cuisinart. No instructions or recipe book came with this processor, so we are not sure of all its features. In addition to the lid-operated on/off, this machine also has an on/off switch and pulse switch. Thus there were several safety features to get in order before starting the machine: the bowl and cover had to be in the correct position, the cover had to be turned to the on position, and the switch had to be on.

A quiet machine, the Merit chopped meat beautifully, sliced hard and soft foods well, even chopped parsley perfectly. It sat firmly on the counter through all operations except grating Parmesan cheese (with the steel blade) and then moved only at the beginning. This drawback could be overcome by adding the chunks of hard cheese after the motor was running. The Merit did slow almost to a half on yeast dough after 3-1/2 cups of flour had been added (the stronger machines can take four to five). It did not stall or cut out. This might indicate that there is no overload cut-off feature, but since there were no instructions accompanying it we couldn't be sure. The only disadvantage we found was that heavy, sticky mixtures (yeast doughs in particular) could get up inside the shaft of the steel blade, making cleaning a less-than-pleasant task. The motor has a lifetime warranty. Other than the lack of instructions, this is a very acceptable machine.

Norelco Food Processor HB1115

This processor has the same blades as most of the others: slicing, shredding, steel chopping and plastic mixing, along with an on/off/pulse switch. It has an automatic cut off feature, a direct drive motor, but no braking action on the blades. It performed well on our tests, although it did not handle raw or cooked meat quite as well as the Cuisinart. The Norelco processor comes with an interesting assortment of recipes and has a hollow pusher that is graduated so you can use it as a measuring cup. Easy to clean and use, we rate the Norelco as a quite satisfactory processor.

General Electric FP-2

Hamilton Beach 707

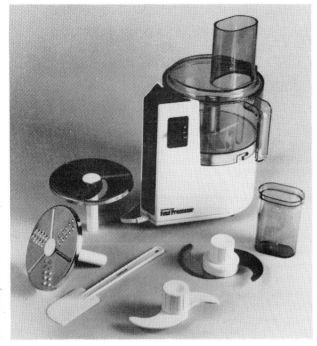

Norelco HB1115

Omnichef Food Processor

Made in France by the same people as the Cuisinart, Omnichef has a more reasonable price tag, but less reasonable performance. The Omnichef has several mimeographed sheets of directions and a handy pocketbook of recipes. It has slicing and shredding discs and a metal blade. It sliced, shredded and chopped well and handled mixing chores beautifully. We found the slicing and shredding discs very difficult to remove after use. The edges of the discs were not rounded, but almost sharp.

Its disadvantage, and a big one, is the switch arrangement. To turn the machine on, the bowl must be in place and then the top is turned by pushing the feed chute (just as on other processors that do not have an on/off switch). However, we found the switch activated by the lip of the top to be quite temperamental and uneven in operation. Also, when the machine is running, the bowl and top move just enough to move the lip away from the switch so the motor turns off. The Lexan bowl has ears rather than a handle, and screws into the base much like a jar lid, rather than simply turning into place. We sometimes had a hard time unscrewing the bowl. Although it handled all functions well, we do not find the Omnichef acceptable because of the difficulties with the switch.

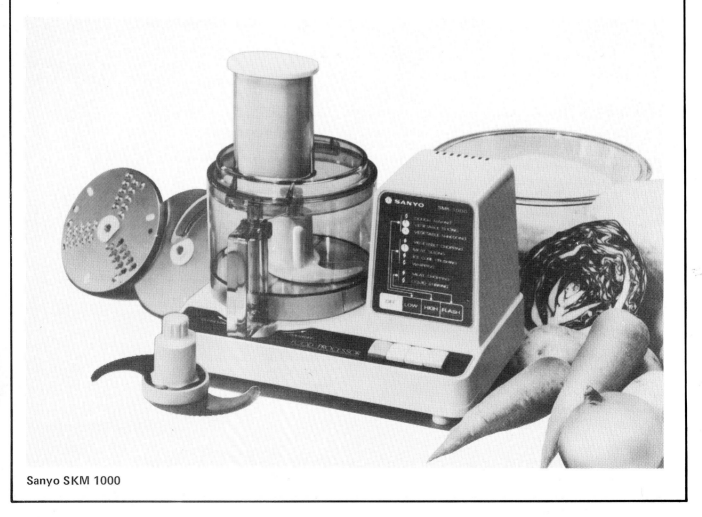

Sanyo SKM 1000

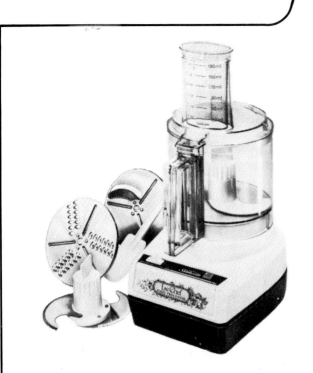

Sunbeam Le Chef 14-11

Sanyo Food Factory SKM 1000

The Food Factory is an apt name for this nifty little processor. It is small, low (the better to fit under a cabinet), belt-driven and has an overload cut-off.

The Sanyo has two unique and worthwhile features: suction feet to hold it firmly in place on the counter and two speeds for better control of the processing action. We found the lower speed especially nice for slicing vegetables and cheese.

The overall performance of the Sanyo was excellent. The only drawbacks we found were the smaller than usual processing bowl, which also restricts the amount of dough it can handle, and the tight-fitting pusher. If yours is a small household then the size of the bowl isn't any problem. The pusher's fit sometimes creates a suction in the feed tube, making it a little inconvenient to get the pusher out. Sanyo also provides a handy cleaning tool that looks like a giant toothbrush. It really does help get the blades clean.

The Sanyo comes with the usual food processing blades (steel and plastic), slicing and shredding discs. Sanyo recommends the plastic blade for yeast doughs, puréeing and general mixing chores. On most other machines the steel blade does this job, but Sanyo's plastic one performed well. We tried a single-loaf bread recipe in the Sanyo (3 cups of flour) and it handled the dough nicely, even though the Sanyo's introductory instructions say to use no more than 1 cup of flour at a time.

Sanyo says their machine can whip egg whites, but only thoroughly chilled ones. Experts say room temperature egg whites whip best—we agree, and we also agree that a beater is still best for this job.

The accompanying recipe book has good basic directions and a nice processing chart.

Sunbeam Le Chef Food Processor 14-11

This heavy, high-quality food processor is among the best we tested. It has direct drive, a braking feature, comes with four blades (slicing, shredding, metal and plastic), has a hollow pusher that is graduated so you can use it as a measuring cup, an automatic cut-off feature, a signal light and three-way switch. The signal light shows you when the unit is plugged in. It is a nice extra feature, but not a necessary one. The switch has on/off/pulse positions and, as with all processors, it will not work unless the cover is locked in place. The Sunbeam Le Chef comes with an excellent guide chart on what blade to use on what type of food. The Le Chef can handle raw and cooked meat, unlike many other processors. We particularly liked the extra big, 2-1/2 quart container that allows you to process larger than usual loads. Le Chef did a fine job in all our tests. Our only problem came with a heavier than usual yeast dough (the type that stalled all other machines)—when it got to be too much for Le Chef it blew a 15 amp fuse. But the fault was really ours, because we overreached the directions for processing yeast dough. We recommend Le Chef.

Waring Food Processor FP510-1

This machine has a lifetime motor warranty, pulse control, braking feature, tandem blade action, a tool caddy, a ready light to show when the cover is in place, a measuring cup in the food pusher and an overload cut off. All of these features have merit, we think, except the tandem blade action, which is nice but not a big deal. The machine comes with lengthy directions. There is an on/off switch in addition to the cover lock feature.

Waring FP510-1

The Waring processor also comes with a special little gadget to tighten the blades in place and then loosen them. We had a hard time keeping track of the little gadget; it could easily slip down a garbage disposal or just disappear into counter clutter if not closely watched. The Waring processor's feed chute is at the back of the machine as you face it, and the handle is at the left, inconvenient placements, we think, except for southpaws. The handle placement is not as much of a nuisance as the chute at the back because, when working on a shallow counter top, or one with an overhanging cupboard, it can be difficult to put food into the feed tube. However, the tube is slightly bigger than some of the other processors, making it easier to get large pieces of food in. At the same time, the larger tube means you have to pack in a bigger load of food, such as carrots or beans. In general, uniform slices depend on packing food tightly in the feed tube.

The Waring processor handles all the common functions well. It did a particularly good job on yeast doughs, stalling only when the full amount (5-1/2 to 6 cups) of flour was added and completely mixed in. Adding the flour through the tube at the back of the machine was the only difficulty.

The instruction book is clear and simple, but has little in the way of recipes. Altogether the Waring is an acceptable food processor.

Welco FP-1 Food Processor

The Welco FP-1 comes with steel chopping, shredding and slicing blades. It has an automatic overload cut-off, direct drive, on/off switch located on the top and a dishwasher-safe bowl. However, it has no braking action.

The machine's performance was acceptable, though it "walked" when slicing hard foods such as carrots or partially frozen meat. When pressure was applied to the pusher during the shredding of cheddar cheese, it stalled.

Handy protectors for safety slide on the steel chopping blade. The lock and unlock positions are clearly marked on the machine top and instructions for meat chopping and dough kneading are marked on the base. They are useful for beginners.

Although the instruction booklet is slim, it contains a good description of basic methods and 14 pages of recipes.

Welco FP-1

Index